Discipleship, Suffering and Racial Justice
Mission in a Pandemic World

Israel Oluwole Olofinjana

regnum

First published 2021 by Regnum Books International

Regnum is an imprint of the Oxford Centre for Mission Studies
St. Philip and St. James Church
Woodstock Road, Oxford OX2 6HR, UK
www.ocms.ac.uk/regnum

09 08 07 06 05 04 03 7 6 5 4 3 2 1

British Library Cataloguing in Publication Data. A catalogue record for this book is available from the British Library.

ISBN: 978-1-5064-8894-3
eBook ISBN: 978-1-5064-8895-0

Typeset in Candara by Words by Design.

Cover design by Joseph Ola | www.josephkolawole.org

The publication of this volume is made possible through the financial assistance of Evangelisches Missionswerk.

Distributed by 1517 Media in the US, Canada, India, and Brazil

Dedication

This book is dedicated to Rev. Dr Joel Edwards CBE (1951–2021) who inspired some of the ideas in this book.

Contents

About the Book

This book explores the subject of discipleship, suffering and racial justice and what the UK church can learn about these themes from the experiences and theologies of Majority World contexts. It argues powerfully that suffering is relative (relativity of suffering) and develops this as a discipleship theory needed during the pandemic and post-pandemic context. The book therefore examines post-colonial contextual theologies rooted in pain and how they can serve the Church during and post-pandemic. It proposes alternative discipleship models that address racial justice concerns using the concept of Jubilee as a theological framework. It argues passionately that mission in today's world must include the concerns of racial justice.

The book explores as an example the suffering context of the pandemic and how the pandemic has affected every area of life. It is argued that this new existential reality is a paradigm shift that demands fresh perspectives and insights on the church's discipleship model and mission engagement.

The book covers a range of themes that will interest many readers: these include discipleship, human identity, racial justice, how to develop an intercultural church or ministry, multi-ethnic Christianity, climate justice concerns, the impact of the pandemic on churches and society, suffering, lament and World Christianity.

Introduction

This book explores the relationship between discipleship and suffering, with a particular focus on how churches in the UK disciple people during the suffering context of the pandemic and post-pandemic. The book critiques Western models of discipleship shaped by colonial and Enlightenment thinking and argues for the need to consider Jesus' discipleship model of suffering and sacrifice. Jesus suffered and died on the cross so that humanity can be saved. He encouraged his disciples to deny themselves and carry their own cross. This constitutes Jesus' paradigm for whole-life discipleship needed in the context of a global pandemic. The book further argues that Western models of discipleship influenced by colonial thinking are very weak on issues of racial justice concerns. It proposes that Majority World Christians (Africans, African Caribbeans, Asians and Latin Americans), due to historic suffering shaped by enslavement and colonialism, have insights and perspectives needed on racial justice issues.

The book develops a Jubilee theology as a framework to bridge the gap of racial justice concerns that seem to be missing in

Western discipleship models. The Jubilee framework as an overarching theme relating to other theological ideas is used to shape some of the conversations on discipleship, suffering and justice.

The deadly virus has created a context of global suffering and has impacted everyone everywhere. It has been on a global scale, affecting at the time of writing 221 countries, causing multiple deaths, loss of community, loss of jobs, increased mental health issues and heightened anxiety and fear. It has brought unparalleled suffering to millions of people around the world and therefore begs the question, how can the global Church, but particularly how can the church in the UK, respond to this global suffering? Perhaps more succinctly, how can the global Church do mission in a context of suffering and loss?

In addition, Covid-19 has affected every area of life, including politics, health, medicine, business, sports, education, entertainment industries, media and of course the Church! If Covid-19 has brought a change in every endeavour of life, which will last for some years to come, has it then ushered in a new paradigm that will require a new model of discipleship and mission? Before the pandemic, I had been reflecting on how the Church, particularly in the Western context, does discipleship and its relation to Jesus' idea of suffering and sacrifice. This question was intensified with the sudden, extended, enforced sabbatical (lockdown), personal suffering and witnessing a lot of pain and trauma that the world is experiencing. The book contends that if the global Church is going to minister relevantly and intelligently in this new context of pain and loss, then we must understand

and apply Jesus' hallmarks of discipleship in the principles of suffering and sacrifice in our various discipleship models.

This book therefore argues using Jesus' model of discipleship of suffering and sacrifice and proposes the need to engage Majority World theologies, whose experience of historic and contemporary suffering is a template for a discipleship model rooted in loss and pain. This template of historic suffering is an essential ingredient in grappling with the realities of the Covid-19 context, and in decolonising Western models of discipleship and mission.

Purpose of the Book

Following on from this brief introduction, the book is written with the following objectives:

1. To highlight Jesus' discipleship model of suffering and sacrifice and propose alternative discipleship models embedded in systemic and structural suffering, looking at experiences from the Majority World.
2. To explore and develop a theological framework on a discipleship model shaped through the lens of racial justice.
3. To argue that the pandemic context is reframing and reshaping how we interpret our existential reality, therefore exploring whether the pandemic context has led to a new paradigm that requires a new model of discipleship.
4. To begin to map out reflections on, responses to and practical applications for the impact of the pandemic.

These four objectives are unpacked throughout the book. The first chapter explores overarching themes by setting the approach and theological framework in the Jubilee concept in the Old Testament. This theological framework is used in reflecting and developing key ideas throughout the book, such as discipleship, lament, racial justice and ecological concerns. Chapter one also explores the theology of discipleship by considering Jesus' model of discipleship in the principles of suffering and sacrifice. Jesus' followers in the early history of the Church also followed this principle to the extent that martyrdom, the idea of dying for the cause of Christ, became a vehicle in propagating the gospel. The global Church can only minister in a relevant way if we firstly understand that we serve a suffering God who calls us to carry our own cross and that, secondly, we have ample examples of the heritage of suffering in the history of the Church. It is unpacking the notion of a suffering God through Jesus Christ, who commands his followers to follow in his steps, that chapter one of this book is devoted. It is argued that this is the basis of whole-life discipleship. This gives the work in chapter two some theorising, theological reflections and analysis on the various themes considered.

Chapter two explores how the pandemic is reframing our reality and tackles the question, if Covid-19 has impacted every sphere of our world, has it then become a new paradigm? But the problem is that it is difficult to conceive of a virus as a paradigm. Nevertheless, could the results, consequences, impact and effect the virus is having on our world and our responses be considered a new paradigm because they have shifted our thoughts? For example, before the pandemic, we had issues of poverty, the climate crisis, racism and other social justice issues; the difference with the pandemic is that it has forced the Church and society at large to gaze at these issues in a new light, thus raising new questions and insights. In essence, the pandemic context appears to have become a new social analytical framework in which we measure our existential reality. If this is true, the implication is that the global Church, and in particular the UK church, needs to rethink its model of discipleship, which is rooted in a Western worldview and paradigms influenced by Enlightenment thinking. For that to happen, Christians in the UK need to look afresh and draw inspiration from Jesus' model of discipleship shaped by humility and sacrifice. The sacrificial experiences of Majority World Christians are a helpful example in decolonising our discipleship models that are heavily influenced by Western dominance and thought.

Chapter three further develops this argument by firstly articulating that suffering is relative (relativity of suffering). It then argues that historic injustices such as slavery, colonialism and their legacies mean that Majority World people are always suffering. If these arguments are valid, the book then proposes that the experiences and contextual theologies of Majority World Christians are templates that elucidate Jesus' discipleship model of suffering and sacrifice. Chapter three further gives the practical implications of this by considering some insights and perspectives on how church networks, mission organisations and theological colleges can engage with multi-ethnic Christianity and racial justice concerns. At the end of each chapter are questions for individuals or small group discussions, which can be used in a local church setting, theological college classes, mission agencies or outside the local church context.

Audience of the Book

This book is written for mission practitioners such as church leaders, CEOs of church networks, para-church organisations and mission agencies who are wrestling with issues of how to position racial justice concerns alongside discipleship and mission. There are ongoing conversations about Black Lives Matter, Critical Race Theory and how best the Western church should respond in this season. It is hoped that this book will help facilitate such conversations. Theological and mission students will also find it very useful because it addresses different theological and mission-related questions.

This book is also written for the UK church, that is, church congregations who are struggling as a result of the pandemic and are asking questions about the relevance of their faith at this critical time and how to engage racial justice concerns that have come into focus. Therefore, it is essentially a work of Practical Theology, providing critical theological reflection on the professional and ministerial practice of the Church. I have used the word Church in capital letters throughout this book when referring to the global Church to denote the general catholicity of the Church (that is, Church Universal). I have used lower case for church where it is a regional, national, or local church such as the UK church and Western churches.

Lastly, this book is written for Christians who are searching for book resources that explore discipleship through the prism of racial justice. There are not many discipleship materials out there in the UK church that address what discipleship that is shaped by racial justice looks like.[1]

The chapters in this book are divided and summarised as follows:

Chapter One: Jesus' Discipleship Model of Suffering and Sacrifice: Hallmarks of Discipleship. This chapter sets the context for what is to follow in the other chapters by exploring discipleship and suffering. It considers the theology of discipleship and suffering from the biblical text and church history, arguing that suffering has always been an integral part of Jesus' model of discipleship and that of his followers.

Chapter Two: The Pandemic Context as a New Paradigm for Mission: Reflections, Responses and Practical Applications. Chapter two builds on chapter one of the book by looking at the suffering context of the pandemic as an example that necessitates the significance of Jesus' model of discipleship shaped by suffering. The main argument of the chapter is that, because Covid-19 and its consequences have challenged and changed everything we know, the Corona-context is considered a paradigm that is shining new light on old issues. It is therefore acting as a decolonising tool, forcing Church and society to engage with some legacies of colonialism.

The chapter explores the impact of the pandemic on humanity through the following themes: human existence and being, human identity, racial justice and Black Lives Matter, sabbath,

---

[1] Chine McDonald's book *God is Not a White Man: And Other Revelations* (London: Hodder & Stoughton, 2021) and Ben Lindsay's book and accompanying podcast on *We Need to Talk About Race* (London: SPCK, 2019) are excellent examples of a few book resources on racial justice and discipleship.

climate justice and its intersectionality with racial justice, the church and the pandemic, mission and the pandemic, theology of suffering and theology of hope. It examines these subjects through theological reflections, responses and practical applications.

Chapter Three: Perspectives of Majority World Theologies on Discipleship and Mission. This chapter articulates that, because of the historic and contemporary sufferings of the Majority World context, this provides an example of discipleship models rooted in suffering and sacrifice. It gives examples of how church networks and mission agencies can adapt their mission strategies and thinking to reflect Majority World theologies and experiences.

Chapter Four: Concluding Reflections: Post-Covid-19 Church. This concluding chapter highlights the key arguments from the book. But, more importantly, it briefly discusses the implications of a post-pandemic Church if we can begin to imagine a post-Covid context.

Significance of the Book

This book is significant because it adds to the debate on the theme of discipleship and suffering by positing that, due to the historic and systemic suffering of people from the Majority World, there is something about the nature of a suffering church that the global Church can learn from Majority World Christians.

Another significance is that, while this small monograph addresses issues that have been around for a while, such as racial injustice, multi-ethnic Christianity and climate change, it is important because it explores a global topical issue in the coronavirus pandemic and how it is changing how we approach some of these themes. Whilst there are lots of people and organisations writing books and articles about the pandemic,[2] there are not many written by Africans; therefore, this makes an original contribution by sharing different perspectives on the pandemic. This work explores the pandemic as an example of a context of suffering from the angle of discipleship, suffering and racial justice. It probes and argues that the UK church needed during and post-Covid-19 is one that operates from a marginal post-Christendom context. It has to be a church that follows Jesus' discipleship model of suffering and sacrifice that can minister in such a context effectively.

The book is important because it will be one of the few books published on the pandemic, further developing the idea of a

---

[2] These are some recent works already on the subject of the pandemic. See Shiluinla Jamir, *Embracing God's Beloved Community: Rethinking Mission in Asia during COVID-19 and Beyond* (Asia: CMS, 2020), https://www.asiacms.net/news/asiacms-proudly-presents-a-new-book-on-rethinking-mission-in-asia-during-covid-19-and-beyond/ (accessed 13 February 2021), John Lennox, *Where is God in a Coronavirus World?* (Epson, England: Good Books Company, 2020), Tom Wright, *God and the Pandemic: A Christian Reflection on the Coronavirus and its Aftermath* (London: SPCK, 2020). Lausanne Global Analysis have also published Kirst Rievan, 'In a Pandemic, Should Missionaries Leave or Stay? A Mental Model for the Missiology of Risk', *Lausanne Global Analysis* 9:4 (July 2020), https://lausanne.org/content/lga/2020-07/in-a-pandemic-should-missionaries-leave-or-stay (accessed 23 August 2020). Operation World have also published: Jason Mandryk, *Global Transmission, Global Mission: The Impact and Implications of the COVID-19 Pandemic* (2020). World Evangelical Alliance have also produced in their journal different reflections on the pandemic including Ebenezer Yaw Blasu, 'The Invisible Global War: An African "Theocological" Assessment', *Evangelical Review of Theology* 44:4 (2020), pp. 302-12.

Corona-theology; that is, our theological reflections and responses to the pandemic context.

The book is also important because it is written by an African practical theologian resident in the UK but writing from the perspective of the Majority World.

Furthermore, the book is of significance because it combines theological reflections on racial justice, exploring its intersectionality with climate justice issues. These are current global topics in the wake of the murder of George Floyd.

Research Methodology

The research method used for this book has been somewhat different, reflecting the pandemic context. Part of it has been done through one-to-one informal phone conversations with church leaders and pastors who are friends and colleagues. This has provided an understanding of shared experiences of how church leaders, churches, para-church organisations, mission agencies and theological colleges are responding to the impact of the pandemic. Church leaders in this context, therefore, refer to those that lead church congregations, but there are also some that work for a Christian charity, para-church organisation, mission agency or theological college. In addition to phone calls with colleagues and friends, I have also participated in Zoom sessions organised for church leaders from two different church traditions. These Zoom sessions have been mainly with Baptist and Pentecostal ministers but there have been others who would identify with independent evangelical and charismatic churches. The period in which I have participated in these Zoom sessions has been from March to July 2020, with some additional observations from August to December 2020. The majority of the Zoom sessions have been with church leaders in the UK, but I have also participated in Zoom sessions with church leaders in Nigeria, Ghana, Peru, the United States and European countries including Germany, Spain, Norway, Sweden, Denmark and France. This has afforded me the opportunity to have a little understanding of the global impact of the pandemic on the mission of the Church. The average age of the church leaders on the Zoom calls has been around fifty. The churches also vary in size; some will be considered large churches with 300 or more church members, while the majority will be small (under twenty members) or medium-size churches with around sixty or more church members. The majority of the churches are in the urban context, while a few are in the rural areas.

In these Zoom sessions pastors shared their experiences of how their churches are adapting and adjusting to online services as well as caring for their congregations or organisations. The sharing also includes the various online platforms being used, as well as how churches are seeking to do discipleship and mission. One could argue that these Zoom sessions are very similar to focus groups because they bring together a group of participants who have a common characteristic in their lives to discuss a research topic.[3] The common factor in all the Zoom sessions I participated in is the fact we were all church leaders involved in ministry. The research topic or topic of interest is how churches

---

[3] Helen Cameron and Catherine Duce, *Researching Practice in Ministry and Mission: A Companion* (London: SCM Press, 2013), p. 109.

and para-church organisations are responding to the challenges and opportunities arising from the pandemic context. Each Zoom session has an average of eight pastors. On other occasions we have twenty or more church leaders, which begs the question whether one can still refer to those sessions with higher numbers as focus groups. The Zoom sessions also act as a place to bounce off ideas with each other and refine views in response to one another. I have gained and learned a lot from those Zoom sessions. A noted limitation of focus groups is that participants might say what people want to hear, therefore obscuring the truth or reality.[4] It is not impossible that, in the Zoom sessions I participated in, in the bid to impress each other about who is making the most of the virtual church services or using the best online platform, the church leaders might have embellished their conversations.

Limitations of the Book

Firstly, this book is limited in scope because it is a small monograph and therefore does not address all questions relating to the subject of discipleship, suffering and racial justice. Secondly, whilst the word Church is used most of the time in capital letters to denote the global Church, in actual sense I am writing from the context of the UK church, addressing challenges and issues within that context. This therefore makes it a work of contextual theology. Lastly is the fact that, whilst employing critical tools from Majority World theologies and perspectives, I am writing primarily as an African practical theologian resident

---

[4] Cameron and Duce, *Researching Practice*, p. 118.

in the UK. Therefore, my perspectives and experiences are only one out of the multiplicity of insights and experiences of Majority World Christians. It is also worth mentioning that, in proposing the experiences and theologies emanating from the Majority World context as examples the Western church can learn from, I have sometimes essentialised or idealised these perspectives. It is therefore important to highlight that Majority World theologies and experiences are not perfect.

Chapter One
Jesus' Discipleship Model of Suffering and Sacrifice: Hallmarks of Discipleship

What is Discipleship?[5]

Any meaningful discussion on discipleship must start with the understanding of the lordship of Christ. This is because it is within this context that we can talk about following Jesus in obedience, dedicating our lives to God's kingdom. The lordship of Jesus as the Messiah who came to us as a vulnerable human being to inaugurate God's kingdom on earth is the central theme of the New Testament. Jesus' idea of the kingdom of God was a radical message in that a worldly king and kingdom in his day were displayed through pomp and pageantry, but the kingdom Jesus introduced was defined by love, submission, humility and peace. This was because Jesus emptied himself, or more

[5] A preliminary version of this section was first published in May 2020 as an article on the Hope 15:13 website: https://hope1513.com/2020/05/06/coronavirus-a-new-paradigm-for-discipleship-and-mission-by-rev-israel-oluwole-olofinjana/. A slightly longer version was published in the *Baptists Together* magazine. See Israel Olofinjana, 'Discerning the Prophetic: Perspective of Majority World Theologies on Suffering and Sacrifice', *Baptists Together* magazine,
https://www.baptist.org.uk/Articles/587272/Discerning_the_prophetic.aspx (accessed 15 September 2020).

accurately did not cling or hold on to power (see Phil. 2:5-7). This is known as *kenosis* (Greek word for emptying oneself), a theological concept that describes the humility and liminality of Jesus' life, ministry and mission. Therefore, Jesus taught that those who want to be great or lead must become a servant in order to lead effectively (see Mark 10:34-45). The implication is that, for Christians to incarnate Jesus' mission, we must first empty ourselves or renounce any worldly notions of power or ambition. This is true to the New Testament idea of leadership or greatness, which can only be accomplished by humility, submission and servanthood. Growing up as a Christian in Nigeria, I remember an experience when I was serving God to be seen by the pastor in the church. There were also times when I was participating in church activities so that I could be promoted to the leadership team of the church. The good thing was that I was not promoted, which upset me even more and I even left the church for a while. But through that frustration, over time and with the help of mature believers from the church, I came to the understanding that we serve God not because of power or position but because he has called us to love and serve him. This experience of powerlessness resonates with the experiences of some of the pastors in some of the Zoom conversations I participated in. This is because many expressed that the pandemic challenged their notions of received power and influence. The pandemic challenged their positional leadership.

The crucial question I have been wrestling with is, if Jesus' way of life includes suffering and sacrifice, how can the Western church discipleship models revolve around these concepts? To begin to unpack this, I will start with an understanding of discipleship that allows the lordship of Christ to reign in every area and sphere of our life. One interesting encounter I had once was with a Christian lady who did not want to talk about church matters outside church services. Her exact words were: 'Let's leave church talk to church services'. This is perhaps a classic example of a narrow understanding of what it means to follow Jesus with all our heart and soul. One of the ways African Christians express discipleship is through the names they sometimes give to their businesses. Take for example grocery shops named God's Blessings or Grace of God grocery shop. Such practices instantly bridge the gap between what is workplace and what is church, what is sacred space and what is secular. In the Western context there has been a whole movement of the church towards expressing discipleship through whole life, in the workplace and public sphere. The work of the London Institute for Contemporary Christianity (LICC) is a pioneering example in this regard.[6] The following parameters are used in this book to define the implications of discipleship that is rooted and shaped by suffering and sacrifice, allowing the lordship of Christ to reign in every area and sphere of our life:

> It is about how the idea of humility and sacrifice is integrated into all of life and not just in some aspects of our lives (not putting our lives into separate compartments). Jesus as the sovereign Lord of our lives must reign supreme in every area and aspect of our lives. This is what it means

---

[6] See John Stott's classic *Issues Facing Christians Today* (London: HarperCollins, 1984), Mark Greene's *Thank God it's Monday: Ministry in the Workplace* (Bletchley: Scripture Union, 2001) and *Fruitfulness on the Frontline: Making a Difference Where You Are* (Nottingham: IVP, 2014).

to love the Lord with all our heart, soul, strength and mind (Deut. 6:5; Luke 10:27).

It is about making following Jesus a lifestyle from Sunday to Saturday (living for him 24/7). The biblical understanding of discipleship is inherently whole-life. Jesus instructs those who were keen to follow him of the cost of discipleship, that they must be ready to prioritise following him above family and possessions (see Luke 9:57-62; 14:25-33). Perhaps it is our modern-day discipleship that has the need to prefix the word whole-life to make this clearer to people.

It is about understanding that, without discipleship, mission will eventually fail (discipleship leads to mission, not the other way round). It is not until our lives are transformed, and priorities re-aligned with God's purposes, that we can replicate that in others. The instruction in the great commission was to make disciples of all nations (Matt. 28:18-20). That is, to incarnate the gospel values in different communities.

It is also understanding that mission is not a programme or event but, rather, mission starts with who we are (being before doing). God's mission starts with a reconfiguring of our identity in him. This is a transformation of our character and purpose of existence in the light of God's mission.

It is choosing to live intentionally for God's mission even when it is not convenient or comfortable. This is knowing and counting the cost of discipleship. Jesus made this very clear when he said to the person who volunteered to follow him: 'Foxes have holes and birds of the air have nests: but *the Son of Man has nowhere to lay his head' (Luke 9:57-58, NRSV). This means we do not follow Jesus for material possession or when it is convenient for us. Following Jesus means we will be inconvenienced.*

It is understanding that being disciples is not only for church leaders or a special few, it is what we are all called to be (missionary disciples). Every Christian in every nation is called to be an apprentice of Jesus, to learn from him, to listen to him and to participate in his kingdom. We are all living stones who contribute to the building and royal priests so that we can all proclaim his kingdom (1 Pet. 2:4-9).

As Christians we want to be followers of Jesus but only when it is convenient or when we are benefitting from the relationship. However, Jesus' imperative calling to his disciples was, if anyone will follow me, they must deny themselves and carry the cross (paraphrasing Matt. 16:24; Mark 8:34; Luke 9:23). I did remember in Nigeria when I gave my life to Christ. It soon became very clear to me that I could not continue to keep company with my friends who wanted me to keep partying, amongst other things. It was a painful realisation for me that, in order to submit to the lordship of Christ in my life, I had to let go of some of my friends. In essence, I had to sacrifice friendship with my friends for a deeper, meaningful relationship with the Lord. This was very difficult to do but, given the circumstances, it was the right thing to do at that time.

Denying ourselves in a consumerist, materialistic and individualistic society involves a lot of suffering, and carrying the cross means we are ready to sacrifice to the point of death for the sake of God's kingdom. Jesus himself demonstrated this as a suffering servant who paid the ultimate price on the cross. What some of the nurses did during the pandemic in carrying out their vocation by sleeping in hotels away from their families, and carers staying at care homes during the lockdown, exemplifies this kind of sacrifice.

The implication of Jesus' suffering is that our discipleship programmes and events, if not preparing people to understand the idea of suffering and sacrifice, will mean they will only follow Jesus temporarily when all is going well. The result is that people will follow Jesus for a while and, when things get really tough, will walk out on God. Another implication is that we follow Jesus as the only lifestyle and not as an optional lifestyle when it is convenient and comfortable. Some of the pastors in the Zoom conversations did express in different ways how members of their congregations were wrestling with what it means to follow Jesus during the pandemic. Some of the members of their congregations find it very difficult, especially when you are losing loved ones or a job, or not feeling well. It is putting every part of us – mind, will and emotions and all aspects of our lives, job, family, education, hobbies, finances – before God to use as he pleases and whenever he calls us. After Jesus gave some serious teaching about what it means to believe and follow him, many of the Jews left him, but then he asked the disciples one important question: 'So Jesus asked the twelve, "Do you also wish to go away?"' (John 6:67, NRSV). Peter's answer to that question is very important for our discipleship today because it demonstrates loyalty and obedience to the lordship of Christ. 'Simon Peter answered him, "Lord, to whom can we go?" You have the words of eternal life' (John 6:68, *NRSV*). Peter's answer is conditioned on the understanding that following Jesus, even when it is rough and difficult, is not an optional lifestyle, but that his very own survival depends on it.

When Christians see discipleship not as some form of alternative lifestyle, but know that our very survival depends on it, this changes the narrative. Take for example the impact of the pandemic on Christians in Africa, who live in abject poverty with the only option of getting any medical help being to pay a heavy financial cost (this is also the case in North America). In such an environment the only option available for their survival is to absolutely depend on God to either provide for their medical bills or miraculously heal them. This experience is different from that of Christians and non-Christians who live in the UK; although they suffer severely from coronavirus, they do not have to pay medical bills and expenses in order to be treated for the virus. There is no doubt that people in the West suffer, through various situations such as terminal illness, disease, depression, loneliness or grief, compounded by the impact of the pandemic on healthcare systems and human interaction. Everyone is suffering from knock-on effects of the pandemic and its restrictions, because the pandemic impacts us all. But this example is to illustrate something of a discipleship that sees following God as the only option, because life itself depends on God for everyday survival. It also illustrates something about the difference in the context of discipleship in the Majority World and the West. I shall return to this in chapter three when developing the relativity of suffering.

Jesus' notion of suffering and sacrifice as an essential element in following him has been demonstrated through the history of the Church. Eusebius, the church historian, chronicles the sufferings and martyrdom of the early disciples and how the Church expanded through persecution in its first 300 years.[7] Many of the early disciples of Jesus suffered in different ways and ultimately sacrificed their lives in following God's call to incarnate his kingdom. An example is James, the lord's brother who was recorded as having been thrown down from the parapet and then afterwards beaten to death with a fuller's club.[8] Martyrdom, that is, the idea of dying for the cause of Christ, was a major theme in early and Patristic Christianity. It also became a vehicle for advancing God's kingdom so that Tertullian (c. 150–225 CE), an African church father and theologian, could say: 'the blood of the martyrs is the seed of the Church'.[9] In essence, martyrdom and mission went hand in hand. Martyrdom is a heavy subject that looks at death from a different vantage point, but I am exploring it here to illustrate the attitude to suffering and sacrifices that the early followers of Jesus had to endure in order to do God's mission.

---

[7] Eusebius, *The History of the Church from Christ to Constantine* (trans. G.A.Williamson; Harmondsworth: Penguin Books, 1965).

[8] Eusebius, *History of the Church*, p. 36.

[9] Tertullian, *Apology*, book 50, in John Foxe and M. Hobart Seymour, *The Acts and Monuments of the Church: Containing the History and Sufferings of the Martyrs*, Part 1 (London: Charter House, 1838), p. 44.

The Reformation period also witnessed several Protestant Christians imprisoned, with confessions beaten out of them, tortured, exiled, excommunicated and killed for their new conviction of following Jesus, at the hands of the official Church. But as soon as Protestantism was established in Europe, there was a reversal so that Catholic Christians were burnt at the stake, hunted, tortured and killed for their beliefs. In the twentieth century, the Communist regime in Eastern Europe, in an attempt to wipe out the church, targeted the Orthodox churches by burning their churches, raiding monasteries and bringing priests and lay people to trial for crimes against the state. This eventually led to a massive number of Orthodox priests and bishops being killed. A new law in 1929 was passed, the Law on Religious Associations, which stipulated that religious groups must register with the government. This law affected Orthodox and evangelicals alike and led to the confiscation and closure of several churches and the imprisonment of believers. Jews suffered horrifically; Messianic Jews also suffered at this period in history because they became targets of both the Nazi and Communist regimes. Examples are Richard and Sabina Wurmbrand, who risked their lives to witness for Christ, enduring terrible torture at the hands of the Communist power in Romania.[10] We also have the example of the underground church in China who were heavily persecuted, imprisoned and tortured for their faith in Christ. One could argue that one of the reasons Christianity has spread in China is because of the suffering of the underground church. In summary, Jesus suffered

---

[10] Richard Wurmbrand, *Tortured for Christ* (London: Hodder & Stoughton, 2004 [1940]).

and sacrificed himself on the cross, and his followers through the most part of the history of Christianity have followed a similar pattern in doing mission. If Jesus' notion of discipleship involves suffering and sacrifice, then why is it that these are not emphasised in our modern Western whole-life discipleship programmes?

Critique of Western Models of Discipleship

Modern theology[11] and mission rooted in the Enlightenment traditions have for so long shaped Western discipleship models. The result is discipleship models that are dichotomised and influenced by the myth of progress. One of the weaknesses of Western models of discipleship is that firstly, they are individualistic. While the Reformation of Martin Luther shifted Christianity from being a faith for the few to everyone, the long-term consequence was that Christianity became personal and individualised. The idea of personal faith and relationship with God, whilst important, should never become individualistic. Our personal faith in God should always be balanced in tension with the communal aspects of Christianity. A second weakness of Western models of discipleship is a follow up from the first. When faith becomes individualistic it can become inwardly focused and detached from the realities around us. This could mean having Christians who love Jesus and want to share the gospel through evangelism but are not thinking of how their faith can serve their

---

[11] Modern theology is the theological enterprise that developed within the European context of the Enlightenment period in the eighteenth century. It sought to engage with the intellectual reasoning of that time.

community or connect with their community. Christianity then becomes a mechanism that serves and is relevant to the church community but irrelevant to the demographics of the church. When faith is conceived as a private endeavour it becomes divorced from public life and civic duties. While some Western evangelical institutions and organisations have developed models of discipleship with a robust public theology and leadership to address this issue, there are still others who focus inwardly. American prosperity gospel preaching comes to mind in this case, when a church prospers and continues to seek prosperity for its members but not for the community at large. This prosperity problem is also seen with some African Pentecostal churches, whose leaders prosper at the expense of their congregation, or the church community prospers but the community at large remains poor.

A third weakness is when our discipleship models are over-spiritualised to the extent of disengaging with political or socio-economic concerns. This happens when churches view climate or racial justice concerns as socio-political issues that the church should not engage with. I have heard on many occasions churches that have an excellent whole-life discipleship programme saying they do not want to talk about race or climate concerns because they are perceived as left-wing politics. Some Western Christians view the concerns of race and climate as social justice issues or wokeness, that is, the idea of being aware or progressive on these subjects. The sad thing is that the history of Western evangelicals demonstrates that social and political action was achieved alongside preaching the gospel, but there was a period in evangelical history when social and political action was seen as social gospel identified with liberal Christians. An evangelical scholar, Derek Tidball, puts it this way:

> *The challenge of increasing secularisation called forth new responses. Straight gospel preaching alone did not seem adequate to cope with the increasingly complex problems of a modern industrial society. Many adopted a solution which was eventually rejected by evangelicals. That was to turn the gospel into a social gospel. Although social concern was originally closely connected with evangelicalism, the social gospel movement became more identified with liberalism.*[12]

The consequences of these weaknesses are a pattern of discipleship that compartmentalises, so that Christianity appears to be relevant on Sunday but not on Monday to Friday at work or the marketplace. A Christianity that purports to doing God's mission but yet fails to engage in climate conversations; a Christianity that separates the sacred from the secular and centres mission only on preaching the gospel through evangelism. In addition, the consumerist feature of modern/post-modern life has also shaped Western discipleship models with the idea of options, progress and greed. It always amazes me when I hear sometimes what people are considering when looking for a church. Does that church have a worship band? What type of songs do they sing? Sometimes it feels like people are in a shopping mall when looking for a church, as they hop from one church to another searching for the right worship band or

---

[12] Derek Tidball, *Who are the Evangelicals? Tracing the Roots of the Modern Day Movement* (London: Harper Collins, 1994), p. 63.

preacher. While the emerging church of the post-modern context, with the model of discipleship premised on whole life expressed through missional communities,[13] has challenged this previous model of discipleship shaped by consumerism, it has not, however, completely been deconstructed. This is where Michael Stroope's (an American mission theologian) penetrating analysis of the language of mission as problematic because of its lack of use in the biblical text and its link to conquest and colonialism is very useful.[14] While not abandoning the language of mission yet, Stroope's thesis is useful in the sense that it allows us to decolonise mission and discipleship.

But what do we mean by decolonisation? This is a term that has increasingly gained usage in our vocabulary. Decolonisation refers to that process in history where indigenous people who were colonised by European powers in Africa, Asia, Latin America and the Caribbean fought for their emancipation from colonial rule. It is a critical theory that studies and analyses the impact of the colonial enterprise on indigenous people and the resistance developed by indigenous people to regain their consciousness and national identity in order to experience freedom from colonial thought and systems.[15] It can be applied

---

[13] Missional communities as defined by the Gospel and Our Culture Network are communities called to represent the compassion, justice, and peace of the reign of God. The distinctive characteristic of such is that the Holy Spirit creates and sustains them. See Darrell L. Guder (ed.), *Missional Church: A Vision for the Sending of the Church in North America* (Grand Rapids, MI: Eerdmans, 1998), p. 142. [See comment for footnote 57]

[14] Michael Stroope, *Transcending Mission: The Eclipse of a Modern Tradition* (London: Apollos, 2017).

[15] For further studies on decolonisation, a good place to start is with some of Frantz Fanon's works such as *Black Skin, White Masks* (New York: Grove Press, 1952) and *The*

to theological education in a Majority World context in the sense of taking an overview of the shift in culture from Christendom to a post-Christian world and looking at what kind of theological education and training are needed for the Church to operate from the margins in a post-Christendom, Majority World context.[16] From a Western context, decolonising theological education involves looking critically at issues of staff recruitment, recommended reading lists, libraries, and subjects being taught. It seeks to ask the following questions: who are the people teaching in our seminaries, theological colleges and Bible colleges? Who are the people writing the recommended textbooks used in our teaching modules and courses? What kind of subjects are being taught in our theological colleges? For the purposes of this book, I am applying decolonisation to discipleship and mission to emphasise the voices and perspectives of Majority World Christians and theologies because Western thought has for years shaped and therefore colonised our understanding of mission. Decolonising mission is therefore used in this book to look at how Majority World Christians understand and practise discipleship and mission that are rooted in suffering and liminality.

In order for Western models of discipleship to be decolonised, an outsider's perspective that is not shaped by an Enlightenment worldview is necessary. This is because one cannot see beyond one's own paradigm. This is where the insights of some of the

---

Wretched of the Earth (New York: Weidenfeld, 1961).

[16] Martin Accad, 'Theological Education as Formation for Prophetic Ministry', https://abtslebanon.org/2019/08/01/theological-education-as-formation-for-prophetic-ministry-2/ (accessed 27 December 2020).

Majority World Christians are needed. For example, George Floyd's death has really exposed that our Western models of discipleship are very weak on racial justice concerns and therefore people in our churches were not fully prepared to engage in such conversations until forced to by Floyd's sudden death. Modern theology, which forms the basis for Western models of discipleship and mission, is not strong on issues of racial justice because it has operated for the most part of it from colonial perspectives. The missionary movement of the eighteenth century that went from the West to the Majority World operated alongside colonial authorities and under the guise of empire.[17] That is why the concepts of Christianity, Commerce and Civilisation were promoted as part of the missionary strategy. Western Christianity needs the voices of Majority World Christians and theologies on discipleship and mission to bring a post-colonial insight and critique from their experiences of colonial suffering. My whole experience as a missionary sent from Nigeria to the UK is full of what it means to be a missionary from below.[18] It took about three years to qualify for a visa and that was after an appeal. I remember my first interview in 2003 at the British Embassy in Lagos, Nigeria. I was dressed in a sharp blue suit for the occasion, naively waiting for something good to come out of the interview. The person that interviewed me, after a series of questions,

---

[17] A recent discussion on the modern missionary movement and its impact on African cultures can be found in Harvey Kwiyani's 'Mission After George Floyd: On White Supremacy, Colonialism and World Christianity', *Journal of Theology and Mission* 36:3, (2020), https://churchmissionsociety.org/resources/mission-after-george-floyd-on-white-supremacy-colonialism-and-world-christianity-harvey-kwiyani-anvil-vol-36-issue-3/ (accessed 29 April 2021).

[18] Samuel Escobar, *The New Global Mission: The Gospel from Everywhere to Everyone* (Downers Grove, IL: IVP Academic, 2003), p. 18.

concluded that I was running away from the country and denied giving me a visa. I was disillusioned for weeks at the conclusion. After appealing the decision, I eventually came to the UK with £20 in my pocket and no financial support from my church in Nigeria, despite being sent. I was also detained at Schiphol airport in Amsterdam because I was on a transit visa and could not afford the direct flight to the UK. When I finally arrived in the UK, I had to build trust with churches before being allowed to preach and teach. No one was willing to suddenly allow an immigrant boy from Nigeria to start preaching; besides, I had not been CRB-checked (what we now call a DBS check). This experience is very different from that of an American missionary that regularly visits my Pentecostal church in Nigeria. He did not have any visa issues. We did not really know him, but he was welcomed with open arms, preaching, teaching and participating in the life of the church and other churches. It is this kind of experience, of othering as a missionary from below, that shapes Majority World perspectives on discipleship and mission.

Another reason why our Western models of discipleship are weak on racial justice concerns is a follow up from the above point, and what I have already alluded to, the over-spiritualised theology that leads to a false dichotomy that somehow separates or compartmentalises our discipleship from racial justice concerns. How can we begin to address this gap in Western discipleship models?

Jubilee as a Theological Framework
for Discipleship and Racial Justice

The concept of Jubilee in the Old Testament (see Lev. 25) gives us a theological framework to help address the deficiencies in Western models of discipleship. This is because the Jubilee framework speaks to the covenant community, economic equality and care for the earth. In essence, the Jubilee framework offers a holistic theological framework that can address the gaps of individualism, privatised faith and lack of racial justice engagement in Western discipleship models. Jubilee is best understood against the backdrop of the children of Israel coming out of Egyptian enslavement, and the new community of Israel understanding its new identity in a covenant relationship with God. In this covenant relationship, God promises freedom for all humanity (Israel as an example) and creation in the fiftieth year. Jubilee provides us with three ideas: Liberty (slaves and prisoners are free), Economic Justice (debts and loans at interest are cancelled) and Ecological Recovery (the land has rest). Prophet Isaiah developed this idea in a messianic figure when he envisioned a just society that provides holistic freedom (Isa. 61:1-2). Lastly, Jesus used the Isaiah text as the basis of his Nazareth Manifesto to shape his Kingdom Theology (Luke 4:18-19). The covenant aspect of Jubilee is a very powerful tool in addressing the individualistic and inward focus of some Western models of discipleship. It gives a framework for a community that is in active relationship with God through a covenant relationship. This should be the basis for discipleship. But note that this covenant relationship is not just for the community of believers to enjoy passively; rather, it is an active covenant relationship that has at the heart of it freedom for slaves, economic equality and ecological concerns. The implication is that discipleship should never be dichotomised from justice issues. One of the strengths of the Jubilee framework is that it connects to other theological ideas such as creation, when it talks about the necessity for the land to rest and recover in the seventh year. The pandemic has really highlighted ecological concerns and therefore the church in the UK cannot afford to be inward and say it is a political issue because the Jubilee framework makes it a theological and missional issue. I will return to ecological concerns in the second chapter.

The Jubilee framework also foreshadows the messianic kingdom when the Messiah will establish God's kingdom on earth. This notion of God's kingdom has the tension of the present reality as expressed in Jesus' Nazareth Manifesto, but also hangs on consummation, when that future kingdom is realised in hope. I shall explore later in chapter two this theology of hope as it relates to suffering and the last days. The debt cancellation of Jubilee is also symbolic of God's forgiveness provided to humanity through the cross of Christ. This encapsulates God's love and forgiveness. This speaks about reconciliation, which is much needed in racial justice conversations. I shall explore this in chapters two and three.

The Jubilee framework therefore furnishes us with such rich theological paradigms like covenant community, creation, justice, God's kingdom, forgiveness, love and hope. As already noted, the Jubilee framework hangs on a covenant relationship with God in the light of justice. In essence, it is about following and developing a relationship with God, but that covenant relationship is not complete until there is justice for the enslaved, or those that are not economically free, or ecological recovery for the land. The emphasis of justice as a key goal of discipleship is what contextual post-colonial theologies such as Black Theology[19] and African Political Theology[20] are known for. Black Theology in the context of apartheid South Africa fought for racial justice for blacks and coloured people.[21] It fought for their political freedom, human identity and dignity, articulating that they are created in God's image. In the British context, Black British theologians such as Kate Coleman, Robert Beckford, Anthony Reddie, David Muir, Dulcie Dixon McKenzie, Pauline Muir, Eleasah Phoenix Louis, to name a few, have all been arguing before the murder of George Floyd for the UK church to take the concerns of racial justice very seriously. For example, Robert Beckford's thesis, known as the Dread Thesis, offers Pentecostal churches a political theology that speaks prophetically to social

---

[19] Black Theology as defined by James Cone, who is regarded as a pioneering father: 'Black Theology is a theology of liberation because it is a theology which arises from an identification with the oppressed blacks of America, seeking to interpret the gospel of Jesus in the light of the black condition. It believes that the liberation of the black community is God's liberation.' James H. Cone, *A Black Theology of Liberation*, 20th Anniversary Edition (Maryknoll, NY: Orbis Books), pp. 4-5. Black Theology also exists in the context of Southern Africa. We also now have Black British Theology in the UK.

[20] African Political Theology is a theology of liberation speaking to the socio-economic and political issues on the continent of Africa. It seeks to address issues such as military coups, political dictatorships, oppression, exploitation, poverty, diseases and environmental issues. See John Parratt, *Reinventing Christianity: African Theology Today* (Cambridge: Eerdmans, 1995).

[21] Basil Moore (ed.), *Black Theology: The South African Voice* (London: C. Hurst & Co., 1973).

and political life in Britain.[22] One area in which African Political Theology and Black Theology offer the UK church a critical tool to engage is the use of lament as an essential ingredient for justice.

Lament and Justice

The theology of lament is very useful as it helps us as Christians to understand that some of the questions people are asking about justice are coming from grief, anger and frustration; therefore, we must allow people to lament and mourn. This is seen very clearly in the Psalms, where the children of Israel will cry out to God in anger and sorrow in troubled times, asking questions. An example is Psalm 13, an individual lament: 'How long, O Lord? Will you forget me forever? How long will you hide your face from me? How long must I bear pain in my soul, and have sorrow in my heart all day long?' (Ps. 13:1-2, *NRSV*). This is also seen in the New Testament in the story of Lazarus's death and his sisters' reaction. Lazarus's sisters, Mary and Martha, did say to Jesus, Lord, if you have come, we would not have lost our brother (paraphrasing John 11:21 and 32). What is more crucial in this story is that, as Mary began to weep, Jesus also started to weep (John 11:32-35). In this story Jesus offers something about the need to allow people to lament and us to lament with them.

Lament as a significant aspect of the theology of suffering offers a process that can help people journey from suffering to justice. Therefore, lament could be a very powerful tool that leads to hope

---

[22] Robert Beckford, *Jesus is Dread: Black Theology and Black Culture in Britain* (London: Darton, Longman & Todd, 1998) and Robert Beckford, *Dread and Pentecostal: A Political Theology for the Black Church in Britain* (London: SPCK, 2000).

and action. Following the tragic death of his sister to Covid-19, Moses Zikusoka, a member of Woolwich Central Baptist Church, launched a memorial project called UK African Covid-19 Experience.[23] The vision of the project is to create an online memorial for people who have lost a loved one due to Covid-19 or related causes, to share information and celebrate the lives of their loved ones. Moses is now a community champion in Greenwich, telling his story to help with the vaccination campaign.[24] This is where lament can be seen as hope, resistance and justice. Cathy Ross, a contextual theologian who works for the Church Mission Society (CMS), has this to say about lament as resistance and justice:

> Lament is also a form of agency. A cry of anguish is not only a way of naming and mourning what is lost but is also a way of standing in the midst of the suffering. And so lament deepens our engagement with the world of suffering and invites us into more active social and political engagement.[25]

Perhaps, if as God's people we lament together, we will begin to hope together and possibly open our eyes to some of the social and political injustices in our systems, such as the police

[23] UK African COVID-19 Experience, http://www.ukafricancovidexp.org/ (accessed 1 October 2020).

[24] NHS Vaccine Facts, 'I had the vaccine because I want to be there for my sons', https://www.nhsvaccinefacts.com/stories/i-had-the-vaccine-for-my-sons (accessed 28 May 2021).

[25] Cathy Ross, 'Lament and Hope', *ANVIL: Journal of Theology and Mission* 34:1 (2018), https://churchmissionsociety.org/resources/lament-and-hope-cathy-ross-anvil-vol-34-issue-1/ (accessed 6 May 2020).

demonisation and brutalisation of African Americans as expressed in the murder of George Floyd. The world is lamenting over the murder of George Floyd and others who have died as a result of police brutality. It is the response to these deaths as typified by George Floyd that has led to the resurgence of the Black Lives Matter protests around the world.[26] One glimmer of hope from these protests is the conviction and sentencing of Derek Chauvin for the murder of George Floyd. This is the start of racial justice, not the end. It is interesting that, in seeking to understand the reasons for some of the Black Lives Matter protests in the UK, Boris Johnson, the UK prime minister, commissioned a report on Race and Ethnic Disparities. The recommendations and conclusions of the report are controversial. Here is an excerpt from the report:

> Put simply we no longer see a Britain where the system is deliberately rigged against ethnic minorities. The impediments and disparities do exist, they are varied, and ironically very few of them are directly to do with racism. Too often 'racism' is the catch-all explanation and can be simply implicitly accepted rather than explicitly examined.
>
> The evidence shows that geography, family influence, socio-economic background, culture and religion have more significant impact on life chances than the existence of racism. That said, we take the reality of racism seriously and we do not deny that it is a real force in the UK.

---

[26] Sadly, some of the early protests became violent and others turned into looting, distracting from the cause of social justice. Nevertheless, George Floyd's death has ushered in a new consciousness on issues of racial justice.

The Commission was keen to gain a more forensic and rigorous understanding of underlying causes of disparities. However, we have argued for the use of the term 'institutional racism' to be applied only when deep-seated racism can be proven on a systemic level and not be used as a general catch-all phrase for any microaggression, witting or unwitting.[27]

The reaction to the report by the general public has been one of anger, frustration, sadness, disappointment and exhaustion. In essence, many people lamented because they were hoping that the report would begin to map out a road to justice. Many people feel that the outcome of the report was intended to spin a positive narrative about race debates and relations in the UK, and that this could also set a dangerous precedent, drawing us back from the few strides that have been made since the murder of Stephen Lawrence in 1993. If the UK government through this report has arrived at the conclusion that institutional racism does not exist, how is society supposed to account for the Windrush scandal of 2017, the Brexit implications of the rise of dangerous rhetoric around migration, the impact of Covid-19 on people of colour and the rise in anti-Asian hatred due to the origins of the pandemic in China? Black theologians will argue that these examples are clear signs of institutional racism and therefore the need to speak truth to power to challenge the structures that oppress.

---

[27] Commission on Race and Ethnic Disparities, https://www.gov.uk/government/publications/the-report-of-the-commission-on-race-and-ethnic-disparities (accessed 2 April 2021).

A clear example of institutional racism from the points above that also illustrates ongoing lament is the disproportional representation of Black, Asian and Minority Ethnic, the so-called 'BAME people' in the frontline services. These frontline services include bus drivers, carers and nurses. The consequence is that 'BAME people' are four times more likely to die of Covid-19 than white British people.[28] While there are ongoing investigations and academic research is still inconclusive, a 2020 survey conducted by ITV News suggested that discrimination plays an important part in the developing story:

> *Black, Asian and minority ethnic (BAME) medics and healthcare workers say 'systemic discrimination' on the frontline of the coronavirus outbreak may be a factor in the disproportionate number of their colleagues who have died after contracting the virus.*[29]

There are also issues around health inequalities and how 'BAME people' are treated. These are social justice issues already present in our system, but the coronavirus context has brought them to the surface.

---

[28] Robert Booth and Caelainn Barr, 'Black People Four times more likely to die from COVID-19, ONS finds', *Guardian*, 7 May 2020,
https://www.theguardian.com/world/2020/may/07/black-people-four-times-more-likely-to-die-from-covid-19-ons-finds (accessed 7 October 2020).

[29] '"Discrimination" on frontline of Coronavirus outbreak may be factor in disproportionate BAME deaths among NHS staff', ITV News, 13 May 2020,
https://www.itv.com/news/2020-05-13/discrimination-frontline-coronavirus-covid19-black-minority-ethnic-bame-deaths-nhs-racism/ (accessed 14 May 2020).

A Lament on BAME

Speaking about the acronym 'BAME', I found the term deeply problematic way before the government's recommendation to abandon its usage in the commissioned report on race released in 2021.[30] This is the reason I have put it in speech marks. One of the problems with this label is how it is lumping together continents, nationalities, ethnicities, cultures and peoples. BAME could easily suggest that the term is referring to a homogenous group of people, which is far from the truth. Take for example the B in the acronym, which refers to black people; this alone could mean people from Africa, which, by the way, is a continent with fifty-four countries and not a country. In addition, black in the acronym also includes African Caribbeans; again, the Caribbean has several island nations and Jamaica happens to be only one of them. This means Jamaica is not synonymous with the Caribbean. Asia is such a massive continent with different languages, peoples, geography, culture and customs. India alone has around 780 languages. Lastly, it is the Ethnic Minority aspect of the term which does not really say anything. Who is supposed to be the Ethnic Minority? Latin Americans, Australians, New Zealanders, Americans, Eastern Europeans? If we consider alone Latin Americans, who are rather often implied in the term, we have around twenty-one countries in Latin America with different customs, cultures and religious traditions. The second problem with the term BAME is that it makes white a neutral ethnicity by which we measure all others. We have white people and then

---

[30] I started critiquing the term BAME in early 2020. See Commission on Race and Ethnic Disparities.

BAME people. White is also an ethnicity. There are other problems with the term regarding whether BAME people actually see themselves as BAME and who is doing the naming; therefore, for these reasons, I am intentionally using in this book Africans, African Caribbeans, Asians and Latin Americans, people of colour, or people from the Majority World when referring to other continents in the Global South.

In ending this chapter, I have explored discipleship and suffering through Jesus' ministry and some of his followers. Jesus' model of discipleship is shaped by suffering and sacrifice. Western models of discipleship rooted in a colonial paradigm do not give emphasis to suffering, sacrifice and racial justice. This is because of their weaknesses of individualism, inward focus and over-spiritualised theology. The concept of Jubilee in scripture provides the Western church with a rich theological framework rooted in a covenant community that can help to connect discipleship and racial justice concerns. Contextual post-colonial theologies such as African Political Theology and Black British Theology address racial justice concerns and therefore can help us in engaging with racial justice through the theology of lament.

Questions for Individual Reflection or Group Discussions

- What does it mean to follow Jesus in today's culture?
- Discuss in what way you have suffered before and how it has impacted your faith?
- Why is suffering an essential part of following Jesus?

- How is your church or organisation creating safe spaces for people to lament?
- What is the role of racial justice in your church's discipleship programmes?

Chapter Two
The Pandemic Context as a New Paradigm for Mission: Reflections, Responses and Practical Applications

In this second chapter, I want to explore the context of suffering that the pandemic has ushered in as an example to help better situate why Jesus' discipleship hallmarks of suffering and sacrifice are needed. The pandemic and the consequences of how it is reframing how humanity views reality can be perceived as a new paradigm that is changing and challenging everything we know, including politics, business, sports, education, social care, health, medicine, travel, tourism, entertainment and the Church. The pandemic context is also acting as a decoder helping us to decolonise certain discourses and narratives. One area in which the pandemic is already reframing the debate is developmental studies. The notion of Western countries as advanced in terms of development and countries in the southern hemisphere as developing is being challenged through how different nations have responded and are responding to the virus. This is in how some of the so-called developing countries, in the early stages of the pandemic, have managed to keep the virus out or reduce its impact, while the so-called advanced or developed countries struggled to contain the pandemic. This reframing of development is clearly articulated in an article by Maru Mormina (a Senior Researcher in Developmental Studies, University of Oxford) and Ifeanyi Nsofor (a Senior Researcher in Health and Equity, George Washington University):

> *Europe's failure to learn from developing countries is the inevitable consequence of historically ingrained narratives of development and underdevelopment that maintain the idea that the so-called developed world has everything to teach and nothing to learn.*

But if Covid-19 has taught us anything, it's that these times demand that we recalibrate our perceptions of knowledge and expertise. A 'second wave' is already on Europe's doorstep. Many countries in the southern hemisphere are still in the middle of the first. The much talked-up global preparedness agenda will require responses to be handled very differently from what we've seen so far, with global solidarity and cooperation front and centre. A healthy start would be for developed countries to get rid of their 'world-beating' mindset, cultivate the humility to engage with countries they don't normally look towards and learn from them.[31]

Another area in which the impact of the virus is challenging dominant narratives is social justice issues such as poverty, climate change and race relations. To take the latter, before the

---

[31] Maru Mormina and Ifeanyi M Nsofor, 'What developing countries can teach rich countries about how to respond to a pandemic', *The Conversation*, 15 October 2020, https://theconversation.com/what-developing-countries-can-teach-rich-countries-about-how-to-respond-to-a-pandemic-146784 (accessed 25 October 2020).

pandemic, there seemed to be the notion that our world is post-racial, particularly in countries such as the United States, with the instalment of Barack Obama as the forty-fourth president of the country. The murder of George Floyd and the global consciousness around racial injustice has changed that narrative. Although it could be argued that it was the murder of George Floyd that was the game changer and not the pandemic, the lockdown that resulted because of the pandemic made the world become more attuned to this injustice, which has been going on for decades. In effect, the lockdown allowed our world to be more conscious of racial injustices that are embedded in our systems and structures. George Floyd's murder has also emboldened and raised a new black consciousness that is empowering many black leaders, activists, theologians and pastors to speak out and challenge racial injustice inside the church and society. Therefore, George Floyd's symbolic death has uncovered and challenged the view that society is clearly not post-racial and that there is the need for Western institutions, including the UK church, to take a review of its policies and procedures in order to challenge racial injustices in our systems and structures.

This new consciousness on racial justice concerns has led to the Church of England setting up an Anti-Racism Taskforce to combat the sin of racism within the Church of England structures. One of the significant results is the report, *From Lament to Action*, with clear recommendations and timelines for the Church of England to follow to bring about structural and cultural change within its institutions.[32] The Baptist Union and Churches Together

---

[32] Church of England, *From Lament to Action: The Report of the Archbishop's Anti-Racism Taskforce*, Church of England,

in Britain and Ireland have also set up a Racial Justice Advocacy Forum to equip the UK church to tackle racism within the church and society at large. Sarah Everard's murder is another example of a symbolic death during the pandemic that has shone light on social justice issues related to gender justice. Many women have been assaulted and lost their lives in the past to gender-based violence, but Sarah's kidnapping and eventual murder by an off-duty police officer during the pandemic led to massive protests to challenge the system on gender-based violence.

But a question I am wrestling with is, can one really call the changes the virus is having on every endeavour of life a paradigm or are they best described as a phenomenon in the sense of an extraordinary event or occurrence? The changes the virus has caused are not only going to be for months but, with most current projections, years to come; therefore, could they be understood as a phenomenon that is prompting a new paradigm? A factor to also consider is that there are further talks that there could be more waves of the pandemic as new variants surface. If the argument is accepted that the virus, being a global pandemic, is a phenomenon that is ushering in a new way of interpreting our existence, and that is a paradigm, what then is a paradigm? I am using the word paradigm here in the sense of a new understanding of humanity's existential reality. This is not necessarily the new replacing the old and totally discarding the old, but a change in worldviews and how humanity reads and interprets reality. Thus, a paradigm is a lens through which we organise our view of the world. It is a cognitive analytical

https://www.churchofengland.org/sites/default/files/2021-04/FromLamentToAction-report.pdf (accessed 26 April 2021).

framework used in describing our worldview. David Bosch, a South African mission theologian, following the paradigm theory of Thomas Kuhn (an American philosopher), noted the different paradigm shifts in theology and mission as Primitive Christianity, Patristic period, the Middle Ages, the Reformation, the Enlightenment and the Ecumenical era.[33] If the pandemic context is acting as a new framework in which Western society and other parts of the world analyse reality in relation to suffering, and if it is also exposing some legacies of colonialism, what are some of the key questions this suffering context is causing people to ask?

Reflections on, Responses to and Practical Applications of the Impact of the Pandemic

In this section, I want to attempt to highlight some of the key questions that the pandemic context raises. These questions are framed in the light of theological reflections, responses and practical actions. Some of these responses are not particular to people of faith, but common to us all (faith or no faith). In essence, it applies to civil society as well as the Church. But perhaps interpreting through the lens of faith gives a different meaning to the themes covered in this book. Some of these themes are explored through the lens of discipleship, suffering and racial justice. Theological reflections on coronavirus have been described by other theologians, such as a British Baptist pastor, Rev. Dr. Steve Latham, as Corona-theology. Latham stated:

---

[33] David Bosch, *Transforming Mission: Paradigm Shifts in Theology of Mission*, 20th Anniversary Edition (Maryknoll, NY: Orbis Books, 2014), pp. 187-92.

We need a similar intellectual movement today: to conceive the gospel as an alternative to the facile dreams of a consumeristic, humanistic, naturalistic, globalised culture. To this degree, Christianity embodies a dualistic contrast between the 'world' and 'not-the-world'. But the situation also requires that we flesh this out in practical actions, to incarnate an alternative way of life.[34]

What Steve is alluding to here is that, just as during the world wars the loss of life forced European theologians such as Karl Barth, Paul Tillich, Dietrich Bonhoeffer and Jürgen Moltmann to challenge the myth of the progress of modernity that was gaining ground at that time and to articulate what is referred to as a crisis theology, so also the pandemic context challenges us to rethink our theology in a consumerist, materialistic and individualistic Western society.

Here is my own initial attempt at defining Corona-theology, if one can use such a term now. Corona-theology is about how the Church seeks to contextualise its mission and practices to respond to the changes and challenges presented by the Covid-19 context. Below are eight reflections, which are not at all an exhaustive list because there will be other responses and reflections besides these. The eight responses are: existence and being, human identity and racial justice, sabbath, climate justice, church and the pandemic, mission and the pandemic, God with us and the theology of suffering, and last days and theology of hope. These

---

[34] Steve Latham, 'Corona-theology', Jeremiad Essays blog, 23 March 2020, http://jeremiadstevelatham.blogspot.com/2020/03/corona-theology.html (accessed 1 May 2020).

theological reflections are in the form of a commentary and responses as well as practical applications.

Existence and Being

How do we in the West understand our humanity when faced with our vulnerability and weakness? Due to its colonial past and dominance in global politics and economics, the West has little tolerance or cultural space for suffering or hardship. How do we learn how to follow Christ through pain when we are desensitised to it by our culture and our context? Amidst multiple deaths in different countries on different continents, the pandemic forces us to reflect on life and our existence. Brexit was our major concern before in the UK, but with this new threat no one is really talking about Brexiteers and Remainers, but about how we can survive Covid-19 together. It has become an existential threat to our way of life and therefore raises the question of theodicy because people are asking, did God cause or allow coronavirus? To those who see the pandemic as a punitive measure with the view that it is a sign of God's judgement, that raises more questions about God's goodness, because how can a good and loving God allow this amount of suffering and loss? These are serious ongoing questions, which do not require neat, quick answers or solutions. They have to be thought out well and carefully in the context of discipleship and mission. This is where the Western church needs the theology of lament mentioned in chapter one to help us wrestle with God and find hope in his purposes for justice. We also need a better understanding of what it means to be weak, powerless and vulnerable. Some of the pastors in the Zoom session did express their powerlessness when, during the pandemic, they could not visit members of their congregations to offer pastoral care when bereaved of a loved one. Others express frustration of competency due to lack of technical expertise in the church to provide online streaming. Jesus' humanity embodies for us what it means to be vulnerable. This is the essence of the cross because it subverts our notions of power when we think of a crucified God. As hinted at in chapter one, Majority World Christians have a lived experience of powerlessness and weakness due to the historic context of subjugation through enslavement and colonialism. I shall develop this line of thought in chapter three.

Evidence is suggesting that people are now turning to God, either for prayers or to have some perspectives on their crucial questions. A survey commissioned by Tearfund in 2020, polling 2,101 adults in the UK, finds that twenty-four percent of adults say that they have watched or listened to a religious service since the lockdown.[35] This report offers us a window into how people are searching for the divine in all the chaos and suffering that surrounds us now.

Since the lockdown, the global Church has responded by going online through all the various platforms that are available on social media (YouTube, Facebook Live, Zoom sessions, Instagram and so on). What is needed in order to answer some of the ontological questions people are asking is possibly to create

---

[35] Oliver Needham, 'A Quarter of UK Adults Engage in Religious Services Online During Lockdown', 3 May 2020, https://oliverneedham.co.uk/blog/2020/05/a-quarter-of-uk-adults-engage-with-religious-services-online-during-lockdown/ (accessed 4 May 2020).

platforms and forums where people can ask the Church those difficult questions. This has to be done with authenticity that demonstrates that we do not have all the answers but that we are willing to journey with people as we struggle ourselves. We have to possibly structure these forums and platforms into two categories, one for already-churchgoers and another one for those who are searching and seeking. The reason for advocating for two distinct online forums is that, while we are asking similar questions about life, the questions are different, and we must give room for them to be articulated well in an environment in which people feel safe to share without being judged. Having said that, having one platform or forum for both groups could create a dynamic space where there is mutual learning. I am aware that churches are already creating such spaces and forums and will encourage that we continue. An example of a Christian charity that is already involved in creating spaces for people to grief and lament is Care for the Family who, through their bereavement support groups, are providing spaces where people who are feeling lonely because of losing a loved one can share.[36]

Human Identity, Racial Justice and Black Lives Matter (BLM)

As questions about human existence are related to questions about identity, I want to explore our humanity. The pandemic, with the effects of decimating the human population globally, is re-aligning our thoughts on our mortality. If human life is by nature finite, then what makes us human? Another way to frame that question is, if our lives are temporal, what makes them

---

[36] Care for the Family, https://www.careforthefamily.org.uk/Family+life/bereavement-support (accessed 1 October 2020).

valuable or useful? The Evangelical Alliance has initiated the Being Human project to explore what it means to be human in our contemporary society.[37] The question about our humanity is not a new one and one classical example we can draw from is Greek mythologyand literature. Homer's epic poem *The Iliad* wrestles with the questions of mortality and identity. The ten-year war or siege which Homer tells a fraction of introduces us to different characters who battle this question of what makes us human and valuable. For heroes such as Achilles, Hector, Ajax, Penthesilea, Aeneas and Nestor, physical strength and battle skills to fight well are what make them valuable, and therefore become their identity. But Homer explores another human dimension to the story, which is love. For Paris (also known as Alexander), it was falling in love with a beautiful woman named Helen of Sparta that made him feel human. Helen herself has to decide against the odds whether she is Helen of Sparta or Helen of Troy. This is again an identity question. Helen of Sparta means she is reminded of her political marriage to Menelaus the King of Mycenae while Helen of Troy symbolises romance for her, despite the complexities.

But there is another human element that Homer's *Iliad* explores, and that is wisdom. Odysseus typifies this human trait in his cunning, which helped to tip the balance of the war in favour of the Greeks. The god-inspired Trojan horse that assisted the Greeks to win the war was down to Odysseus's craftiness and wisdom. But there is yet another side to the whole story and that is the divine angle in the anthropomorphic interventions of the

---

[37] Evangelical Alliance, Being Human Project, https://www.eauk.org/what-we-do/initiatives/being-human (accessed 31 December 2020).

Olympian gods and goddesses in the saga, such as Aphrodite (the goddess of love) supporting Paris against the other goddesses, and Athena (goddess of war) and Hera (goddess of women, marriage and family), who were enraged with Paris's choice of Aphrodite and therefore vouched their support for the Greeks. Why the details of this story about Greek mythology? Firstly it is to illustrate that questions around human identity are not new. Secondly, the kind of identity questions people were asking in the classical period are similar to some of the identity questions people are asking during the pandemic. A key one that I want to explore, because it relates to issues of suffering and racial justice, is around race and identity. The murder of George Floyd has led to the resurgence of the Black Lives Matter (BLM) protests. The Black Lives Matter movement has become politicised and controversial. Some people view it as controversial because they think saying that Black Lives Matter means saying other lives do not matter. Other people see it as a left-wing political movement with a Marxist ideology.

Let me start to unpack the questions around identity and race by reflecting on the issue theologically. Firstly, an anthropological view of scripture affirms that all, that is, everyone, is created in God's image (see Gen. 1:26; 2:7; 5.1-2). We are all bearers of God's image irrespective of colour, nationality, social status, ethnicity, religion, culture or gender (whether female or male). This means that our humanity is rooted in God; this is different from Homer's view of demi-gods (half god and half human), because our human identity is derived from God. We bear God's image because we are the stamp of his creation; therefore, we can affirm that all lives matter. All lives matter to God and are valuable because we are his handiwork. This contrasts with other ancient creative accounts that pictured humans as either slaves of the gods manipulated and used, or as created as an accident of the gods. Our humanity also bearing semblance to God also reveals a collective human identity, therefore a shared identity. The African philosophy of *ubuntu* makes this point clearer when it says:

> My humanity being caught up, is inextricably bound up to, in theirs. We belong in a bundle of life. We say, 'a person is a person through other people.' It is not 'I think therefore I am.' It says rather: 'I am human because I belong.' I participate, I share.[38]

Ubuntu makes it clear that our human identity is not an individual one but a shared one that is interdependent. This is akin to the covenant community that was explored in the Jubilee framework in chapter one, and is therefore useful in challenging the individualism we see in Western forms of discipleship. In addition, the effect of the virus is making society also realise more than ever before that, if we are going to survive, we have to work together in the face of our mortality. Having established this collective human identity, affirming that all lives do indeed matter, how does the rhetoric of Black Lives Matter factor into this? If it is agreed that all lives do indeed matter and there is a shared understanding that our humanity is rooted in God, then it should concern us all (Christians and non-Christians) when black lives are made cheap. Black lives are made cheap when not

[38] Desmond Tutu, *No Future Without Forgiveness* (London: Random House, 1999), p.35.

seen as human, enslaved, colonised, indentured, raped, exploited, seen as inferior, marginalised, oppressed, lynched, segregated, disproportionately imprisoned, murdered and neo-colonised. Whilst not advocating that the Church believe and follow everything about the Black Lives Matter movement, the best way to understand the message of Black Lives Matter theologically is through Paul's body metaphor: 'If one member suffers, all suffer together with it; if one member is honoured, all rejoice together with it' (1 Cor. 12:26, *NRSV*). Black Lives Matter is saying that people of African descent worldwide, as part of the human race, are suffering from various forms of injustices; therefore, their pain matters. Will our collective humanity seek to understand this pain and respond, or will society neglect that part of the human family? For the global Church, this is an even more pressing theological issue because, if we fail to address the hurt in some part of God's family, that is, the body of Christ, we are inadvertently neglecting ourselves.

But, some Christians will argue, how can the Church engage with Black Lives Matter, which uses Marxist ideology and critical race theory? These are questions of what the Church uses as our sources of theology and how we engage in this debate. But a wider question that people do not often ask in these conversations is, why does critical race theory exist in the first place? Could it be that critical race theory exists in a worldview dominated with the idea that black people are inferior, therefore the consequence of such thinking means society did not really have their best interest at heart when it comes to justice? The American context was enslavement and segregation while the European context was the involvement in the slave trade and colonisation of African countries. None of these 'metanarratives' favour people of colour.

It is therefore not good enough to dismiss Black Lives Matter because it uses critical race theory and Marxist theory. The Church has to engage with Black Lives Matter because it is raising crucial questions on the issues of racial justice, racial justice being understood as strategic thinking and action to combat personal, cultural and institutional racism that dehumanises people of colour who are created in God's image. The Old Testament gave us some insights on how to engage with contexts and cultures that are different from the biblical worldview; for example, Moses took the advice of his father-in-law Jethro on leadership delegation despite the fact that he was a priest of Midian (see Exod. 18). The liberation of the children of Israel from Babylonian exile came as a result of Cyrus, the Persian (see Isa. 45:1-3; Ezra 1:1-4). Esther's story is perhaps more succinct in that, whilst it was a non-Jew (Haman) that plotted their destruction, it was also a non-Jew that delivered them (King Ahasuerus). Paul in the New Testament engaged with Greek literature and philosophy, even quoting from them to make the gospel message relevant to his audience (see Acts 17:23, 28 and Titus 1:1).

The history of Christian theology also reveals that the question of how Christianity engages with culture and secular worldviews is not new. Many of the early Church Fathers debated this; for example, Justin Martyr (c.100–c.165 CE) explored the parallels between Christianity and Platonism, while one of the African Church Fathers, Tertullian (c.160–c.225 CE) asked the question: 'What has Athens to do with Jerusalem? What relevance has the

Platonic Academy for the church?' (in his *De Praescriptione Haereticorum,* or 'On the Rule of the Heretics'). Augustine (354–430 CE), one of the well-known North African bishops, in his writings (*Confessions* and *City of God*) explored what Christian identity and citizenship look like in a Roman pagan culture. Modern theology also wrestled with this question of Christianity and European culture or, to be precise, German theologians such as F.D.E Schleiermacher (1768–1834) and Paul Tillich (1886–1965), in their attempt to make Christianity relevant during the Enlightenment period, engaged the prevailing cultural reasoning of the day. H. Richard Niebuhr's (1919–1962) highly influential book *Christ and Culture* was a continuation of this debate, setting out five approaches to culture: Christ against culture, Christ of culture, Christ above culture, Christ and culture and Christ the transformer of culture.[39]

If the Church is going to be relevant today and be able to speak to racial inequalities, we must seek to engage intelligently with Black Lives Matter even though it uses Marxist ideology and critical race theory. The Church cannot afford to engage with Black Lives Matter from an arm's length. It is important for the Church to engage with Black Lives Matter because it raises the question around the issues of race and identity for many, particularly young people. If the Church is going to make the gospel relevant to millennials and Generation Z, then we have to engage with some of the concerns of Black Lives Matter. During the Windrush period (1940s–1960s), the UK church lost a generation of African Caribbean youth because they saw how the

---

[39] Richard Niebuhr, *Christ and Culture* (New York: Harper and Row, 1951).

UK church mistreated their parents; therefore, many of them turned away and embraced, for example, Rastafarianism, which connects with their identity. If the UK church does not engage with the concerns of Black Lives Matter, we will not only lose black youth, but also white youth and other young people, because Black Lives Matter is a multicultural international movement.

Another critical reason necessary for the UK church to engage with Black Lives Matter is because the UK government's report on Race and Ethnic Disparities has contested that there is not substantial evidence for institutional racism. Although the commissioners have released a statement to clarify and defend their position,[40] the damage appears to have been done. This is because the report contradicts the many lived experiences of Africans, African Caribbeans, Asians and Latin Americans who have suffered from racism and continue to experience racial discrimination and inequalities in society. The UK church, like the prophet Isaiah, has a prophetic role to play at this critical time by envisioning a just society. To make such a vision a reality, firstly, the whole of the UK church in its breadth of diversity needs to be empowered and equipped by the Spirit to tackle and address racial injustice in society. This is because the fight against racism is a collective responsibility. Secondly, the church must empower Africans, African Caribbeans, Asians and Latin Americans to continue to fight the racial discrimination that they face in church and society. This is because the fight against racial injustice is

---

[40] Government Response: Statement from the Commission on Race and Ethnic Disparities, https://www.gov.uk/government/news/the-commission-on-race-and-ethnic-disparities-statement (accessed 4 April 2021).

exhausting, tiring and demoralising, causing all sorts of mental health issues. Lastly, we need to empower Africans, African Caribbeans, Asians and Latin Americans to fulfil their God-given potential and attain human flourishing. This empowering will require, as argued in chapter one, a discipleship model that addresses racial injustices in church and society and seeks to build a better integrated future.

Sabbath

The year 2020 has seen different governments all over the world applying various measures that restrict people's movements. The pandemic, therefore, has forced on society a complex kind of sabbath, or a different pace of life. Christian understanding of sabbath is usually associated with rest or, to borrow Nicola Slee's (a British practical theologian) reflection: 'an alternative to our harried hurried culture'.[41] However, the lockdown measures acting as an enforced sabbatical are not necessarily encouraging people to rest because of several factors. Firstly, many now work from home, which means the balance of work and rest has become very difficult to achieve. Secondly, home schooling means working from home is no longer a straightforward process. Another complexity is the fact that it has not been a time of rest for frontline workers such as nurses, doctors, cleaners, bus drivers, bin collectors, to mention a few, because they have all had to be working extra hours and round the clock during the pandemic. Some nurses have had to stay in hotels or isolate for months and carers live in care homes for months, as their vocation

[41] Nicola Slee, *Sabbath: The Hidden Heartbeat of our Lives* (London: Darton, Longman & Todd, 2019), pp. 1-3.

demands a sacrificial lifestyle. There is something the UK church can learn here about the high level of sacrifice that people's jobs have placed on them and the need to apply them to our models of discipleship. It is also clear from the Zoom conversations that pastors as frontline workers conducting funerals are exhausted from the burdens of ministry.

Other scenarios that lead to the idea of the lockdown as an enforced, prolonged sabbath are elderly people not being able to see their family; disabled people not able to visit relatives; single people locked out of family life completely; homeless people housed in hotels; students locked down in universities, not able to receive lectures or buy food provisions. All these make the idea of considering the lockdown as a time of rest problematic. Reflecting on other experiences from the Majority World context, for those that live in other parts of the world such as Nigeria, the lockdown exacerbates the problem. Take, for example, hawkers and food vendors whose work involves selling food provisions on the side of the road while cars are static because of heavy traffic. This kind of job does not provide the luxury of working from home. Working from home is also problematic because of the lack of or no electricity. For the majority of Nigerians to be able to work from home they would need at least three generators to compensate for when the electricity is off.

To take another reflection from another part of the Majority World, life has become unbearable in some other parts of the world due to increases in food prices and access to medicine. For example, some of the poorest people in Peru are really struggling to survive on a daily basis with no money, food, medicine, basic hygiene and sanitary products. The option of staying at home is not possible because people's survival is conditioned on going out. They know going out is potentially fatal because of the virus but they also know that staying indoors is also risky because of the lack of money and basic needs. This has led to a situation whereby people are dying at home as well as outside as the virus continues to spread.

Rev. Dave Mahon, Co-Director at Nauta Integral Mission Training Centre in Peru, has this to say about the situation: 'People here do not expect any help or support from the government because the structures here are corrupt so that you cannot moan at the government for not helping. People feel abandoned because of failure of colonial governments in the past and successive governments in the present.' He made further comments about poorer families in Peru:

> *Daily survival for an average poor family looks like three generations of Peruvians living together in a household where one or two people have Covid-19 and, because of living conditions, it means social distancing or self-isolation is not possible. This is exacerbated by the fact that someone from the family, usually a younger person, has to go out and get food from the farm or market, which the family have to consume in a day because there is no refrigerator. Added to this is the fact that getting medical help for the people infected is so costly because you need to buy medicine. Because of this, many poor families turn to medical self-help or seek local remedies.*[42]

---

[42] In a one-to-one Zoom conversation with Rev. Dave Mahon.

While the measures and restrictions the pandemic requires have disturbed people mentally, spiritually, psychologically and physically, they are also forcing society to ask the big questions. It is like a reset button has been pushed that forces some parts of the world to slow down and reflect. It has also helped those of us in the West to appreciate our freedom of movement and choice, which we have perhaps taken for granted because there are other parts of the world where this is not freely enjoyed. Viewed positively, could it be that the restrictions that the pandemic requires are forcing us in the West to take a step back and reflect about God, life and other important matters? Can we be still and know that he is God? (Ps. 46:10). The concept of Jubilee in the Old Testament was designed to allow for a reset button. That is why the fiftieth year was designated as a period in which some of the economic injustices were set straight, to allow for a rebalance of society and land. A key part of the Jubilee discourse already mentioned in chapter one is the sabbath rest for the land. The idea of sabbath in scripture has a triple application: God himself rested after his creative works; in similar fashion he ordered that humanity takes time to rest and reset on the seventh day, and lastly is the sabbath rest every seven years for the land. The Jubilee concept therefore provides us with a sabbath principle of rest, reset and reflection. The lockdown periods, albeit problematic in several respects, also facilitated an opportunity for people to spend time with their families and provided windows of rest in a busy, consumer society. Perhaps, they can help Western societies to restore the balance of rest and work instead of a constant pursuit of happiness through unhealthy work patterns. Although it must also be acknowledged that the lockdown brought certain pressures on families in terms of inhabiting a confined space, and reports of domestic abuse have also increased, not only in the UK but in other parts of the world.[43]

Loneliness, which is a form of suffering, is another issue that has increased during and after the lockdown periods. While this is more pronounced with people that live on their own, there are other people who are isolated through mental or emotional issues exacerbated by the pandemic, or those suffering physical illnesses who cannot receive the support which they usually enjoy. There are also those who cannot see any relatives or close friends for a prolonged period because they have been shielding. All these raise the question of mental health and loneliness and how the Church is going to minister in such contexts. One UK church initiative that is already responding to the issues of mental health and loneliness is Kintsugi Hope, founded by Patrick Regan OBE. The mission of Kintsugi is to create spaces where mental and emotional health are well understood, accepted and discussed.[44] But mental health must not be separated from racial injustice. This is because sometimes the impact of racism, exclusion, discrimination and marginalisation on people of colour leads to various health issues such as isolation, depression, rejection, anxiety and loneliness. Again, the UK church in its discipleship

---

[43] Deniz Ertan, Wissam El-Hage, Sarah Thierrée, Hervé Javelot and Coraline Hingray, 'COVID-19: Urgency for Distancing from Domestic Violence', *European Journal of Psychotraumatology* 11:1 (2020); Amber Peterman, Alina Potts, Megan O'Donnell, Kelly Thompson, Niyati Shah, Sabine Oertelt-Prigione and Nicole van Gelder, *Pandemics and Violence against Women and Children*, Centre for Global Development, working paper 528 (2020); Anant Kumar, 'COVID-19 and Domestic Violence: A Possible Public Health Crisis', *Journal of Health Management* 22:2 (2020), pp. 192-96.

[44] Kintsugi Hope, https://www.kintsugihope.com/vision (accessed 28 September 2020).

practices must bridge the gap between mental health issues and racial justice concerns.

The lockdown period viewed positively could also help us in the West to align our priorities and focus on what really matters in life. But the problem the UK church still has is that we are trying to do church in a consumer's way; trying to replicate all the busyness and activities we used to do in the church building, but now online or in a hybrid format. This means transferring all our activities, or some, onto online platforms without asking the question: 'What really works and what doesn't work?' Rather, what we should be doing is taking a step back to reflect and then ask the question: 'What is God saying to us in this season?'

If the UK church can be re-energised and refocused during this season, we will be able to minister afresh to the new challenges and opportunities that have emerged through the coronavirus pandemic. It also looks like God's creation has been groaning, indeed, due to over-consumption and an economic exploitation of the earth's resources. Perhaps Covid-19 is one of these groaning pains to warn humanity of our poor stewardship of God's planet. What is our ecological responsibility to care for God's creation?

Climate Justice and Racial Justice:

Before the coronavirus outbreak, one of the dominant global discourses was the subject of climate change. The year 2020 was supposed to be the COP26 conference, the UN global summit on the climate crisis. Due to the pandemic this has now taken place in November 2021 in Glasgow Scotland. But what was, however, interesting as a result of the pandemic was that there were fewer cars on the road and planes flying; therefore, carbon emissions were reduced during the first lockdown, if only briefly, as things have sadly returned to normal. This was well established by scientists, who mentioned that the first pandemic lockdown helped a little to reduce pollution.[45] A question therefore can be posed: is coronavirus a combatant factor in reducing climate pollution? Is coronavirus acting as a catalyst to enforce a sabbath rest for our planet? The Jubilee framework mentioned in chapter one becomes very significant in the light of a sabbath rest for our planet. In the Old Testament, as discussed above, God instituted among the Israelites a sabbatical rest for the community and the land. The community of Israel was supposed to cultivate the land for six years and then allow the land to rest in the seventh year by not cultivating at all (see Lev. 25). This sabbath principle allowed for an ecological recovery of the land and their agricultural system. It is a difficult question to answer because, on the one hand, the virus has decimated lives and people's livelihoods, but on the other hand, it has also acted as a catalyst in helping us to reflect more about our humanity and our relationship with the environment. Therefore, it looks like the pandemic is helping humanity to understand that some parts of creation have been groaning in pain for a while (Rom. 8:18-23).

The recently released UN report on climate change (IPCC Report) has given the world our starkest warning yet that we are in a fight for survival and the window for saving our planet and future

---

[45] Jonathan Amos, BBC News, 27 March 2020, 'Coronavirus: Lockdown continues to suppress European pollution', https://www.bbc.co.uk/news/science-environment-52065140 (accessed 6 May 2020).

generations is rapidly closing.[46] As our world continues to wrestle with the climate crisis and the pandemic, what role can the Church play in the climate discourse? If the Church is going to play an active prophetic role in the climate conversations, we must seek to mobilise the whole Church. This will mean educating church members through sermons, Bible study series, Sunday school materials and worship songs and liturgy on the need for climate justice. Climate justice in this instance is understood as the shared responsibility of the Church to speak up and act to safeguard the dignity and rights of those disproportionately impacted by climate change. Therefore, the whole Church must view climate justice as an essential part of God's mission. This will in turn help the Church to begin to shape its practices in the light of caring for God's creation. Some church traditions are ahead of others on this because of their active engagement in climate change conversations.

While African countries and the Caribbean islands are disproportionately the victims of environmental crisis, while the climate ambassadors and activists are usually white westerners. The cropping of Vanessa Nakate, a Ugandan climate activist, by the media in a photo shoot has become a symbolic story speaking to this issue.[47] But she is not the only one who felt marginalised because, in another video documentary report by another climate activist, Fatima-Zahra Ibrahim, she explores how climate activists

---

[46] The Intergovernmental Panel on Climate Change (IPCC) Sixth Assessment Report, https://www.ipcc.ch/assessment-report/ar6/ (accessed 13 August 2021).

[47] BBC News, 'Vanessa Nakate: Climate activist hits out at "racist" photo crop', 24 January 2020, https://www.bbc.co.uk/news/world-africa-51242972 (accessed 1 October 2020).

are usually white and middle class, who do not represent white working classes or people from the Majority World.[48]

While the problem of who represents who in the climate activists' movements is ongoing, African and African Caribbean churches and their diaspora churches in Europe are very slow at engaging with the issue of climate change. However, a recent survey poll on views and attitudes of Black British Christians on climate change suggests that they are well informed of the climate crisis due to connections to their countries of origins, where people have experienced the effects of climate change.[49]

In addition, the survey also revealed that Black British Christians are twice as likely to act compared to the British public. While this is quite revealing, demonstrating that Africans and African Caribbean Christians are aware and are doing something about the climate crisis, there is still the need to break down some barriers for a wider engagement. One of these barriers is a theological orientation that does not view ecological issues as an essential part of God's mission. A re-orientating of these churches, particularly the Pentecostal expression, is necessary in order to mobilise the African and African Caribbean churches. What is apparent but yet obscure to African and African Caribbean Pentecostal churches is that a systematic study of African religious traditions and philosophy reveals that African cosmology, that is, African creation accounts and stories, is rich in terms of God caring for creation. The African traditional view of God and creation understands the need

---

[48] BBC News, 'Climate movement does not represent me', 23 September 2020, https://www.bbc.co.uk/news/av/uk-54209707 (1 October 2020).

[49] Joe Ware and Chine McDonald, *Black Lives Matter Everywhere: A Study of Public Attitudes towards Race and Climate Change* (London: Christian Aid, 2020), p. 5.

to protect the community, the land, forests, water and certain animals so as to bring an ecological balance to nature. African and African Caribbean Pentecostal churches will do well to embrace an African Eco-theology of creation that moves us into action in engaging with these conversations.

It is therefore exciting to report that, in seeing this gap, Christian Aid, in partnership with some Black Majority Church pastors, theologians and activists in the UK, have set up a working group to engage with the issues of climate justice.[50] The group understands the following as its role:

Speak out: Acting as a prophetic voice in the climate justice movement. Speaking truth to power for climate justice for the poor from the perspective and experiences of people of colour and faith.

Participate: In a range of activities to ensure the movement fully reflects the ethnic diversity of faith leaders active on this issue. 'This isn't just about black leaders engaging in the movement but enabling the movement to recognise the value of engaging with faith leaders from minority communities.'

Collaborate: Solution focused based on what we can do together to make what isn't working better.

Share good practice: Develop and share good practice that can benefit black faith leaders, Christians and the wider climate justice movement.[51]

---

[50] This working group brings together on a monthly basis Black Majority Church leaders, theologians and activists. I am part of the group.

[51] Christian Aid, 'A Prophetic Journey Towards Climate Justice: Terms of Reference of the Working Group with Black Majority Churches', PowerPoint document, 2020.

This group serves as an example of a collaborative effort in bringing together those already involved in the conversation and a constituent part of the Church that has been missing from the table in engaging with the issues of climate justice. This group addresses climate justice concerns through the understanding that climate justice issues are very connected to racial justice issues. It therefore focuses its work on empowering people of colour so that they can be well represented and engage with climate organisations and conversations.

The Church and the Pandemic

The pandemic context is forcing us as Christians to rethink how we do church and what church actually means. The situation is bringing about the true meaning of the church as expressed in the Greek words *kuriakon* (meaning: belonging to the Lord) and *ekklesia* (meaning: the community of called-out ones or believers). Although the meaning of *kuriakon* later changed to be used in the sense of church buildings, the original meaning was people belonging to the Lord. The fact that churches cannot physically gather together in the way we used to because of a threat to our collective existence is pushing us back to understand that our life is not our own and that we belong to the Lord as a community of called-out ones. More than ever before the Church is cherishing its community of people more than the building, which in some cases dominates our mission. There are books that have been written on how the mission of the Church needs to go beyond maintenance to mission.[52] Pastoral care also takes on a

---

[52] See for example Graham Cray, *Mission-Shaped: Church Planting and Fresh Expressions*

new meaning, as we do this through social media or good old-fashioned phone calls on the landline to congregants who are not on social media or do not have a mobile phone. Christians are rediscovering what church community really means because we are missing fellowship and that sense of belonging. Many of the pastors on some of the Zoom conversations did express the isolation they faced despite having online services. They also expressed the frustration of their congregations with the dislocation caused by hybrid services.

One of the impacts of the Covid-19 context is how it is necessitating the Church to rethink its practices. The Catholic Church, for example, declared that its members could make their confession to God because it was difficult to see a priest to confess.[53] Other churches now do virtual communion services or the Lord's Supper, which raises an important theological question about the meaning of communion. Is a virtual communion service valid, if everyone is offering their own elements of bread and wine? What happens if people present something else other than bread, or a different kind of drink: is that still considered authentic?

---

of Church in a Changing Context (London: Church House Publishing, 2009); Les Isaac, *Relevant Church: A God-given Goal* (London: Ascension Trust, 2004) and Robert Beckford, 'From Maintenance to Mission: Resisting the Bewitchment of Colonial Christianity', in Phyllis Thompson (ed.), *Challenges of Black Pentecostal Leadership in the 21st Century* (London: SPCK, 2013), pp.32-51.

[53] Cindy Wooden, *Crux*, 20 March 2020, 'If you can't go to confession, take your sorrow directly to God, says Pope', https://cruxnow.com/vatican/2020/03/if-you-cant-go-to-confession-take-your-sorrow-directly-to-god-pope-says/ (accessed 29 September 2020).

This is where the Jubilee framework is also useful in helping us to understand that the church community is in a covenant relationship with God. The implication is that communion expresses fundamentally a believer's covenant relationship with God. Our covenant relationship with God has several elements such as accountability, stewardship, community, faithfulness and discipline. It is therefore imperative that the Church as a covenant community, whilst accountable to God, is also accountable to each other. This sort of thinking should underpin our online services so that, even when we are not physically together, we are still disciplined enough and accountable to the community of faith.

Another impact of the pandemic context on the practices of the Church is in the area of finances and giving. A survey conducted during the first lockdown of 2020 by the Evangelical Alliance suggested that nearly half of churches, forty-six percent, are seeing reduced donations.[54] Some churches who depend on renting their building or facilities are now struggling financially. Others whose membership give cash only are also struggling. It appears that, just as the virus is affecting jobs and businesses and causing some to shut down, it is sadly bringing an end to some churches as well. However, it is not all bad news in terms of church finances because the Changing Church survey of the Evangelical Alliance also revealed that the majority of individuals attending churches (seventy-two percent) have maintained or increased their giving.[55]

---

[54] Evangelical Alliance, *Changing Church: Autumn Survey Executive Summary*, https://www.eauk.org/assets/files/downloads/Changing-Church-autumn-survey-executive-summary.pdf (accessed 4 November 2020).

[55] Evangelical Alliance, *Changing Church*.

Another impact of the pandemic on UK churches is that not everyone wants to return to in-person service due to various reasons. Some are still shielding from the virus, while others are still very careful and protective of where they travel. Yet there are also those who have formed the habit of enjoying the consumerist nature of online streaming so that physical church attendance has lost its appeal. There are also those who through the pandemic have become disillusioned with church and life in general. From my observation, only a section of some local congregations has returned. This has led to different models of hybrid services with smaller groups of people returning while others join via online streaming. Some churches favour not returning at all, preferring online services because of how successful their online services have been compared to when they were in a church building. Another reason some churches are not favouring returning into their buildings or rented premises is because their church members are concerned about the spread of the virus and further variants. There are also those who are planting online churches as an avenue to reach the next generation. I will say more about this in the next reflection. Yet some are thinking creatively and structuring their churches into smaller groups, similar to home groups, house churches or Bible study groups. Those that might prefer this latter option could be structured like missional communities where discipleship and mission can connect together. Whatever shape or form our returning into church buildings looks like, a crucial question is, how do we disciple people through this crisis and post-pandemic?

The New Testament church, which followed Jesus' discipleship model of suffering and sacrifice, suffered everything in order to survive and share the gospel. They also operated on limited resources because they were a poor church. Suffering being an integral part of their discipleship model means they were ready for any context. Some of the para-church organisations and churches from the Majority World, due to poverty, persecution and economic recession, are used to discomfort and therefore can teach the church in the UK how to survive in a context of lack and pain. For example, Maggy Barankitse, who suffered torture and witnessed horrific acts during the Burundi genocide in the 1990s, managed to lead a children's sheltered home (called Maison Shalom), which provides healthcare, education and culture to Hutu and Tutsi children.[56] Maison Shalom, despite the context of genocide, provides hope to Hutu and Tutsi children who have been brought up on ethnic hatred. Barankitse's whole-life discipleship model is premised on the love for God that does not abandon the relationship with him when we suffer or experience discomfort. Her discipleship model is also expressed in love that overcomes ethnic hatred and divides, which is why she cared for Hutu and Tutsi children, showing them how to experience God's love and love each other. This para-church organisation can teach the UK church something of how to continue to love God and follow him during the pandemic and post-pandemic, but also how love can be implemented in our racial justice strategies. I will say more on this in the next point.

---

[56] Faith and Leadership, 'Maggie Barankitse: Love made me an inventor', https://www.youtube.com/watch?v=PWSxAA4nOg0 (Accessed 4 May 2021).

Following on from reflecting on the impact of the pandemic on the Church is the impact of the pandemic on the mission of the Church. One of the current challenges for UK churches is that it feels like we are scattered or in dispersion due to the impact of the pandemic. While some of the pastors in the Zoom conversations are enjoying meeting online, others are struggling with the sense of creating two communities as a result of hybrid services. The hybrid nature of streaming and in-person worship can feel like a scattered church. The Old Testament way of understanding the concept of scattering and belonging are the two prophetic trumpets the Israelite community have to use in their wilderness sojournings. One was for gathering together while the other was for scattering (Num. 10:1-10). The impact of the pandemic presents us with a scattering model. Peter also used an interesting term in the New Testament in his letter. He wrote to Christians who were scattered because of persecution: 'Peter, an apostle of Jesus Christ, to the exiles of the Dispersion in Galatia, Cappadocia, Asia and Bithynia' (1 Pet. 1:1, *NRSV*). The word translated 'dispersion' here is the Greek word *diaspora*, which means scattering. The dispersed or scattering model of church means every member has to be equipped and deployed for God's mission. This again raises the question of discipleship and suffering and the readiness to be inconvenienced for the sake of the gospel mentioned in chapter one. The scattering model of church means that as Christians we are all missionary disciples ready to obey the master when he calls us to step out of our comfort zone. But perhaps what can aid the mission of the church during this pandemic season is to understand that the church is not restricted but is deployed.[57] This is a military term denoting troops and equipment being moved into position for action.

Whilst the pandemic context has created challenges for the Church, it has also created opportunities for the mission of the Church. For example, in the UK, we are seeing new ways of connecting with Christians and non-Christians through food and medicines delivery, befriending the elderly and people isolated, a moderate increase in mental health work, debt-counselling support and school support.[58] There are also churches that have opened their buildings to other projects that benefit the wider society, because of its lack of use during the lockdown. For example, some church buildings are being used as vaccination centres. One of the significant developments during the lockdown period was that the various online platforms for streaming Sunday services reached beyond the church walls and perhaps for the first time we have a chance in this post-modern, post-church context to reach people with the gospel we could not reach before. The survey mentioned earlier commissioned by Tearfund discovered that: 'A quarter of adults in the UK have watched or listened to a religious service since the coronavirus lockdown began, and one in twenty have started praying during the crisis'.[59] This indicates that there is an openness and willingness to engage with God. This will require the UK church to be creative and innovative to respond to this openness.

---

[57] This was a phrase I heard two of my Baptist colleagues, Rev. Craig Downes and Rev. Andrew White, use.

[58] Evangelical Alliance, *Changing Church*.

[59] Needham, 'A Quarter of UK Adults...'

One of the sections within the UK church that has been creative and innovative before the pandemic context is the Fresh Expressions of church.[60] Fresh Expressions of church is the attempt of the UK church to be incarnational in doing church for the un-churched. This expression of the church allows for creative thinking as we consider discipleship and mission in a post-Christendom context. Fresh Expressions of church, such as churches planted in housing estate areas, cafe churches, Messy Church[61] and so on, have expressed church in such a way that those that are not Christians can feel comfortable and engage with Christianity. This church movement has ignited the necessity to reach beyond the church walls for a generation that will not step into our church buildings or understand church in traditional settings. However, my observation is that one of the weaknesses of this important church movement is the lack of engagement with racial justice concerns. This is expressed in two ways; one is in the lack of engagement with Black Majority Churches, Asian churches and Latin American churches. A second is that many of the Fresh Expressions key leaders do not speak publicly on racial justice matters nor address them in their discipleship publications. Maggy Barankitse's discipleship model of love that crosses ethnic divides can be very useful here in bridging the

---

[60] For more on Fresh Expressions of church see: Michael Moynagh, *Emergingchurch.intro* (Oxford: Monarch Books, 2004); *Church for Every Context: An Introduction to Theology and Practice* (London: SCM Press, 2012) and *Church in Life: Innovations, Mission and Ecclesiology* (London: SCM Press, 2017).

[61] Messy Church is a form of church that involves children's and adults' creativity, celebration and hospitality. It is primarily a church for people that do not belong to another church. See 'What Messy Church is and isn't', https://www.messychurch.org.uk/what-messy-church-and-isnt (accessed 6 May 2020).

cultural gap so that Fresh Expressions of church can find ways to engage Black Majority Churches, Asian churches and Latin American churches. Barankitse's discipleship model of love that speaks against racial injustice can also help Fresh Expressions leaders take the concerns of racial justice and begin to speak out publicly on these issues as well as write about them in their discipleship programmes. The Jubilee framework discussed in chapter one expresses God's love and forgiveness through debt cancellation, which points towards forgiveness and reconciliation achieved through the cross. This is apt in helping different church communities work towards race reconciliation and speak together on racial justice concerns.

Church Planting and the Pandemic:

Another implication of the pandemic on the mission of the Church is that we are now beginning to see some pastors and church leaders planting churches online. The usual or best practice when it comes to church planting is careful consideration of the context or community into which the church will be planted. There are different models of church planting, such as denominational, collaborative (involving different ecclesial congregations or organisations), intercultural church plants (bringing together ethnically and culturally diverse teams or churches) and incarnational church plants. Whatever model of church planting, they all require certain logistics and planning, such as finding a suitable venue or premises, a small team to start with, finances and visionary leadership. But an online church plant, while employing similar strategies, requires a different kind of approach and planning. Firstly, like in a physical church, planting is to establish the purpose or vision of the church plant. Is it for already-Christians who are disillusioned by the impact of Covid-19 or is it purely missional? Secondly is to explore what online platforms might serve that purpose. For example, if the purpose of the church plant is to reach out to millennials and Generation Z, streaming such services on Facebook will probably not be effective because Generation Z tend to use platforms like Instagram. A third factor is to consider strategies for how to promote this new online church so that it is accessible. Again, this will require careful consideration of how to promote and within which circles. If the purpose of the church plant is to reach non-church people, promoting in media circles that reach only church people will probably defeat that purpose. Another point for consideration is finance and looking at what platform is within the intended budget.

But the advantage of an online church plant is that in the current climate, with people open to spirituality, it can be started easily and in an instant. This is because all the barriers of locating buildings or premises are easily overcome and it is a cheaper way to plant a church. However, this also raises some concerns. Firstly is the fact that some people have really struggled to adjust to life online and prefer a physical community to have that sense of belonging, so this type of church planting could easily overlook the concerns of those who have not warmed up to online platforms. Secondly is that, just like in a physical church plant, anyone who senses God calling them, without the call being properly tested in a community of faith, can start their own church. The difference is that this type of church planting can be started instantly without due diligence and corporate discernment from a covenant community.

Lastly is the key question of discipleship. How do we disciple new believers online in a time of crisis? Going back to the Jubilee framework in chapter one, with the idea of our relationship with God being rooted in covenant, it seems to me that discipling well online during the pandemic and post-pandemic will require a covenant understanding that can hold individuals accountable. This is because it is difficult to monitor people online as people can select which part of church services they participate in. But a proper grounding in covenant theology can help people to be disciplined and remain faithful to God when it is difficult for the community of believers to hold individuals accountable. This will require again an understanding of sacrifice, in the form of sacrificing our personal desires of the temptation to do as we please. Instead, we understand that being in a covenant relationship with God requires fellowship with other believers so that we can grow together. The writer of the letter to the Hebrews expresses the importance of encouraging fellowship with one another and not making a habit of not being in communion with other Christians (see Heb. 10:25).

God with us (Emmanuel) and the Theology of Suffering:

It might seem strange to talk about Christmas in this section, but I am doing this to illustrate a couple of things about the nature of suffering and discipleship. The new strain of the virus that developed towards the end of 2020 resulted in some European countries and other parts of the world to enter what effectively could be described as the third lockdown. The last-minute decision of the UK prime minister, Boris Johnson, to cancel the previous relaxation of the rules to allow families to celebrate Christmas caused a national upset. Some saw this as Christmas having been cancelled, but the question is, what is society's understanding of Christmas? Is Christmas about the commercial and consumerist pattern of shopping? Is it about our various national, regional and family traditions that people have accumulated over time? Is it a holiday when people feel it is a good time to rest because it is the end of the year? That the season set aside for Christmas has become heavily commercialised with consumer gods reigning should not be a surprise, because anyone who understands the history of the Church will know that the original season to celebrate Christmas has only gone back to its pagan origins. The day designated to celebrate the birth of Jesus has its origins on the day the Romans used to celebrate the unconquerable sun (in Latin *Sol Invictus*) as a god that appears during the winter solstice. This idea was introduced or reintroduced to Rome, depending on which scholarship you follow on this, by the Roman emperor Aurelian (214–275 CE) after he defeated Queen Zenobia.[62] This new god, who was also identified with Mithra, a Roman god claimed from the Persians, was celebrated near the shortest day, winter solstice, on 25th December. When Constantine (272–337 CE), the Roman emperor, converted to Christianity or affiliated with it in 312 CE, he began to draw parallels between *Sol Invictus* that the Romans worshipped and Christ the Conqueror (*Christus Victus*) depicted as the Sun of Righteousness mentioned in Malachi 4:2. This initial

---

[62] Edwin Yamauchi, *The World of the First Christians* (Tring: Lion Publishing, 1981).

development eventually led to the Latin Western churches adopting 25th December as the birthdate of Jesus instead of the previously observed 6th January by some churches. This adoption of 25th December is not necessarily a bad idea because no one actually knows the exact birthdate of Jesus. But perhaps what is more crucial is how people celebrate this significant event and what sort of meaning is attributed to it. Christmas has somehow come to mean that people can do almost anything they like and buy anything their hearts desire. Western society uses Christmas as an excuse to encourage consumerist attitudes. People also use it to sanction their innate desires. This is where Jesus' discipleship principle of discipline against greed is very important: 'Then he said to them, "Watch out! Be on your guard against all kinds of greed; life does not consist in an abundance of possessions' (Luke 12:15, *NIV*). Here is Jesus' model of discipleship challenging our consumerist way of life.

Christmas celebrations should be about focusing on the gift that God has given to humanity in Jesus. It should be about serving other people rather than ourselves. Christmas should embody celebrating others by giving gifts to other people without expecting them to return us the same favour. Christmas should be about thinking and helping homeless people, people that are lonely and people that do not have food. It is God's gift to humanity, demonstrating that he is with humanity and that we are not alone because he sacrificially gave us his one and only son as a gift to show us how to live sacrificially. Will the real Christ stand up in the midst of the consumer gods? The question Jesus posed to his disciples at Caesarea Philippi about who do people say that the Son of Man is, is more crucial than ever before (see

Matt. 16:13). Is Jesus just one of the great prophets, a sage or teacher, or is he much more than that?

The pandemic context means the Church also has a window of opportunity to share the gospel of Christ about Emmanuel, that is, God that is with us even when we are lonely and suffering in a pandemic and post-pandemic.

The immanence of God incarnated in Jesus as Emmanuel, that is, the God that comes to us as a vulnerable child but also with hope for humanity, is a crucial message during and post-pandemic. In the days when Jesus was born, Israel as a nation was under the Roman rule and life was made difficult for an average Jew through heavy taxation, poverty and disease. Jesus' birth as the Messiah in that context of oppression signals hope. The Church has this gospel of hope to share during this pandemic and post-pandemic. But a further thought for our discipleship is that Jesus as Emmanuel came to us as a vulnerable baby that needed protection from the political forces of his day that wanted to crush him. His humanity demonstrates weakness, something that we need in our discipleship programmes today. Too often our discipleship programmes lean towards the notion of the divine Son of God that conquered the world through resurrection rather than the Son of Man that comes to us in humility and vulnerability. Jesus' birth as Emmanuel and death on the cross gives us a theological framework for a discipleship rooted in suffering because his birth reveals his vulnerability while his death demonstrates his willingness to suffer and sacrifice himself for the sake of humanity. The Church's discipleship practices should be shaped by these two theological contours of our faith.

I shall return to this theme of suffering and discipleship in chapter three when I further develop reflections on the subject.

Last Days and Theology of Hope:

The last reflection in this chapter is how the pandemic context is causing people to ask the question, is this the end? This question is being asked by people of faith as well as people of no faith. For people of faith, particularly Christians, some are examining the apocalyptic texts in the Bible, such as the book of Zechariah, Daniel, Revelation and the popular Jesus discourse in Matthew 24, in the light of recent world events. Anyone reading Matthew 24 will almost want to conclude that Jesus is living in our time, as the text depicts vividly recent global events. For example, Jesus said in Matthew 24 that nation will rise against nation and that there will be famines and earthquakes in various places (paraphrasing Matt. 24:7). Recent world events, such as the Taliban taking over control of Afghanistan, the drought experienced in some African countries, hurricanes and storms in the Caribbean, the locust plagues in East Africa and New Zealand bushfires, could all elucidate this text, particularly in the light of an eschatological eco-theology. In essence, some of the recent natural disasters could be explained in terms of the environmental crisis we are facing, but yet also make us wonder whether they are the signs or contractions of the last days?

All the millennial theories and rapture theories (if you are a dispensationalist)[63] are being examined in the light of Ebola

---

[63] Dispensationalists are those who read the Bible by breaking it into seven unequal periods of time called dispensations. The last dispensation, which talks about

outbreaks, the Syrian refugee crisis, the presidency of Donald Trump, the climate crisis, Brexit and now coronavirus. Is this indeed the end of the world as prophesied in scripture? Is coronavirus the new Antichrist? The spread of the virus has also led to the spiralling of conspiracy theories, such as linking the genesis of the pandemic in China and other places to the creation of 5G technology, and vaccinations to the mark of the beast mentioned in the book of Revelation (see Rev. 13:17).

Regarding whether this is the end of the world, there are no easy answers and only time will tell. This is where the theology of hope shaped by the resurrection of Jesus becomes very profound. Jesus' suffering and death on the cross provides the Church with a theological framework for the lament and suffering that we are all facing during the pandemic, but the resurrection also provides us with hope for the future. Part of that theology of hope is again rooted in the Jubilee framework, in that God promises to end slavery, economic injustice and ecological recovery for the land. Jesus' kingdom theology, rooted in this understanding, speaks of the year of the Lord's favour (see Luke 4:19), that is, hope and liberty for all. The Church must hold in tension the idea of God's future kingdom and that of his present kingdom. His present kingdom means we must continue to lament and fight for racial justice and climate justice, whilst also knowing that his future kingdom will be a reality one day. I think we are definitely living in uncertain times as we continue to confront the virus and its impact on world economy, politics and health. Perhaps what is more uncertain at the moment are the new variants of the virus

---

humanity being under the reign of Christ, has different theories about the rapture and the millennium.

surfacing and spreading in different parts of the world. The good news, however, is that there are vaccines to combat the virus in Pfizer-BioNTech, Oxford-AstraZeneca, Moderna and others. But opinions are still divided because, whilst many welcome the vaccines, some people are very cynical and sceptical about the vaccination for various reasons. For example, in a recent survey in the UK, it is reported that seventy-two percent of Africans, African Caribbeans and Asians are not likely to take the vaccine, citing lack of trust in the vaccination due to institutional and structural racism.[64] As already mentioned above, linking the vaccination with conspiracy theories creates another barrier in people receiving vaccinations.

But it is good to know from a report by Churches Together in England (CTE) that Pentecostal and Charismatic leaders have either not given room for these conspiracy theories to flourish or have spoken out against them publicly.[65] Church leaders are dealing with these various conspiracy theories by protecting their congregation. Some do this by warning their congregations of dangerous messages that seem to circulate on WhatsApp and on social media platforms. Others engage in a series of Bible study discussions around the last days to give a balanced view and teaching on the second coming of Christ. Some church leaders are

---

[64] Linda Geddes, *The Guardian*, 16 January 2021, 'Covid vaccine: 72% of black people unlikely to have jab, UK survey finds', https://www.theguardian.com/world/2021/jan/16/covid-vaccine-black-people-unlikely-covid-jab-uk?CMP=Share_iOSApp_Other (accessed 17 January 2021).

[65] Churches Together in England, 'Pentecostal and Charismatic Churches and COVID-19', https://cte.org.uk/Articles/579120/Home/Coronavirus/Pentecostal_and_Charismatic.aspx (accessed 1 June 2020).

also engaging the medical profession and politicians to educate their congregation through webinars, online discussions and forums. Some altogether avoid the topic because of lack of confidence in expounding the teachings on the last days. The Church clearly needs a theology of hope that espouses a responsible eschatology that addresses conspiracy theories and fear, but at the same time educates the Church on the role of suffering, lament and hope. Augustine of Hippo, one of the African Church Fathers in early Christian history, speaks of hope in terms of the city of God and the city of the world. The city of the world was dominated by the corruption and evils of the present world in the Roman Empire, while the city of God was God's future kingdom that will reward faithful believers who endure the present persecution. But again, Augustine uses this tension of the yet and not yet to describe Christians' earthly citizenship, which makes them responsible in the city of the world but at the same time live in tension for the future city of God.[66] Responsible eschatology means Christians hold their two citizenships in tension. Our earthly citizenship makes us responsible citizens on earth in terms of caring for God's creation and other responsibilities, but at the same time we know that our hope rests in our other citizenship, the heavenly citizenship. The late René Padilla (1932–2021), a Latin American theologian, puts it this way:

> I argue for a view of the kingdom of God that gives proper weight to Jesus' teaching regarding his own role in the fulfilment of Old Testament prophecy. As a matter of fact,

---

[66] Augustine, *City of God* (trans. Henry Bettenson; London: Penguin Books, 2003).

I said, this is the basic thrust of the New Testament, that in Jesus's person and work the kingdom of God has become a present reality and provides the basis for the mission of the church. Between the times of Christ, the church looks back to the already that has been accomplished through Jesus' first coming and also to the not yet that points to the future completion of God's redemptive purpose at Jesus' second coming.[67]

Whether our church tradition believes that this world will be renewed or recreated, an important matter is discipling people during the pandemic to prepare them for that second coming of Christ. A balanced understanding of the theology of suffering and theology of hope shaping our discipleship should prepare us for his second coming. While personally I think this is not necessarily the end, I think what we are experiencing currently could be a warning and a preparation towards the second coming of Christ.

Questions for Individual Reflection or Group Discussions

- How has the pandemic changed your views on health, politics and faith?
- Discuss how the murder of George Floyd has changed racial politics and race relations and what role should the church play?

---

[67] René Padilla, *Mission Between the Times* (Carlisle: Langham Monographs, 2010), p.10.

- The impact of the pandemic on churches has led to the development of a hybrid model of church; how can the church disciple people during and post-pandemic?
- How will you or your church (workplace) participate in tackling issues of climate justice?
- How should the church seek to engage with Black Lives Matter?

Chapter Three
Perspectives of Majority World Theologies on Discipleship and Mission

*Suffering Conditioned by Historic Injustices:
Relativity of Suffering*

In the first chapter I began by exploring Jesus' discipleship model in the hallmarks of suffering and sacrifice. I argued that this is important for today's Church that is confronted by global suffering expressed in the pandemic. The second chapter has explored how the pandemic is reframing our reality in the light of various reflections and practical applications on different themes and how they relate to discipleship and racial justice. The pandemic has exposed that life is indeed temporal and that suffering and pain are real; therefore, what sort of disciples does the Western church need to disciple others in this context? Part of my argument in chapter one is that the experiences and theologies of Majority World Christians provide Western Christians with some crucial insights to help navigate this context. I want to further develop this thought in this chapter.

The characteristics of the Covid-19 context are uncertainty, despair, suffering, pain, grief, trauma, loss and isolation. It is perhaps the followers of Jesus, who have been prepared through suffering and sacrifice, that are best placed at this time to reach out to people and help them follow Jesus faithfully. The idea of suffering and sacrifice is relative (relativity of suffering), so that what Majority World Christians who are refugees, asylum seekers and economic migrants have suffered (and continue to suffer) will be very different from white, middle-class European Christians. I am not advocating or suggesting that Africans, Asians or Latin Americans have a monopoly on pain and trauma. A notable example of a white European who suffered is the German theologian Jürgen Moltmann, who spent his early years in a prisoner-of-war camp, an experience from which he developed a pioneering approach to the notion of a suffering God.[68] Moltmann's theology of suffering, of a God that suffers through Jesus in a suffering world, is a very powerful reflection needed for this period. But what I am nuancing here is the fact that some Majority World history demonstrates that certain regions of the world have suffered from systemic and institutional injustices like the slave trade, indentured servitude, imperialism, colonialism and neo-colonialism and therefore this makes Majority World Christians accustomed to suffering and pain.

In addition, the legacies of these institutional injustices continue in the lives of so many people from the Majority World today. An example of what African descendants continue to suffer is the Windrush scandal of 2017, which saw immigration control in the

---

[68] Jürgen Moltmann, *The Crucified God* (London: SCM Press, 1974).

UK wrongly detain, deport and deny legal rights to African Caribbean people.[69] Another is the already mentioned disproportional representation of Africans, African Caribbeans, Asians and Latin Americans at the frontline services in such a way that has led to the deaths of many people of colour during the pandemic. While coronavirus affects everyone – whether you are rich or poor, white or black, or even a head of state (Boris Johnson and Donald Trump) – the reality is that it does pose more of a risk to poorer communities, including Africans, African Caribbeans, Asians and Latin Americans.

If the pandemic context is indeed becoming a paradigm, and if the arguments are accepted that people from the Majority World suffer due to historic systemic and structural issues, what then can Western Christians learn from these contexts? Jehu Hanciles, an African theologian and mission thinker, commented on what Western churches can learn from the Majority World voices:

> Fundamentally, the factors and considerations that framed the Western missionary movement – including the idea of Christendom, imperial expansion, political and economic dominance, and technological supremacy – are strikingly absent from the emerging non-Western movement. Where enlightenment certitudes (including the universal relevance of Western ideas and ideals), militarist triumphalism, and a rather secular emphasis on means and human calculations framed the Western movement, it is the experience of colonial domination, marginalization, and an

---

[69] The Windrush generation is referred to as the African-Caribbean migration to the UK from around 1948 to the1960s to help rebuild Britain after the Second World War.

intensely spiritual worldview that will provide the defining elements in the non-Western movement ...   The New Testament emphasis on 'weak things of the world' (1 Corinthians 1:27) will inform the thinking and outlook of non-Western missionaries.[70]

Hanciles is here describing what it looks like to do mission from a vulnerable position as opposed to previous models of mission engaging from a place of power and structure. Building on my arguments in chapter one, this line of inquiry provides the church in the West with a template to learn from Majority World theologies such as Black Theology, on discipleship models rooted in suffering and sacrifice caused by social economic inequality. One of such templates offered is lament, explored in chapter one. Lament is a key theological concept in Black Theology because many of these contextual theologies originate in the context of loss and pain. Another example of a contextual theology shaped by poverty, exploitation and oppression is Liberation Theology, which developed in the socio-economic poverty context of Latin America as the Catholic Church decided to side with the poor and the marginalised.[71] The pioneering and prophetic approach of this theology was the understanding that God is the God of the oppressed and the downtrodden. Therefore, it is a preferential option for the poor and places the exploited at the heart of gospel transformation. The evangelical response in Latin America was sought in integral mission that understood the gospel as

---

[70] Jehu Hanciles, *Beyond Christendom: Globalization, African Migration, and the Transformation of the West* (Maryknoll, NY: Orbis Books, 2008), p. 369.

[71] See as an example, Gustavo Gutiérrez, *A Theology of Liberation* (London: SCM Press, 1974).

expressed in proclamation and demonstration through social responsibility. One of the founding documents in the development of integral mission stated:

> *Taking as a basis the biblical vision of the kingdom of God as the goal of transformation, the document (Wheaton 83 statement) which could be regarded as the strongest evangelical affirmation of commitment to integral mission in the last quarter of the twentieth century, unequivocally affirms that evil is not only in the human heart but also in social structures... The mission of the church includes both the proclamation of the gospel and its demonstration. We must therefore evangelise, respond to immediate human needs, and press for social transformation.*[72]

Integral mission then, offers the Western church a holistic idea of pursuing economic justice and ecological concerns as well evangelism and discipleship. This again resonates with the Jubilee framework developed in the first chapter. Perhaps for those who might find the ideas in Black and Liberation Theology too radical or left wing, integral mission offers an evangelical perspective that is faithful to scripture but at the same time seeks to address political, economic and ecological concerns. As already mentioned in chapter one, Black Theology also emerged in a Southern African context to challenge the systemic injustice caused by the apartheid regime. One of the key concepts in Southern African Black Theology is the *ubuntu* philosophy, which underpins the Truth and Reconciliation Commission in post-

---

[72] Padilla, *Mission Between the Times*, p. 13.

apartheid South Africa. *Ubuntu* pursues racial justice with the understanding of human interdependence. It sought for racial justice through restorative justice that can bring healing and wholeness to the entire community. It exemplifies the New Testament theology of forgiveness and reconciliation with our estranged neighbours. Desmond Tutu, the chair of the Truth and Reconciliation Commission stated:

> I contend that there is another kind of justice, restorative justice, which was characteristic of traditional African jurisprudence. Here the central concern is not retribution or punishment but, in the spirit of ubuntu, the healing of breaches, the redressing of imbalances, the restoration of broken relationships. This kind of justice seeks to rehabilitate both the victim and the perpetrator, who should be given the opportunity to be reintegrated into the community he or she has injured by his or her offence.[73]

Ubuntu therefore gives Western Christians and Majority World Christians residing in the West a discipleship template of pursing racial justice together. In essence, it sees racial justice being achieved through collective responsibility and healing. This is important for multi-ethnic churches and organisations who want to tackle racism together. Nelson Mandela, reflecting on his long years in prison, speaks about the need for the oppressor and the oppressed to be free in order to achieve justice:

> It was during those long and lonely years that my hunger for the freedom of my people became a hunger for the

---

[73] Tutu, *No Future without Forgiveness*, p. 51.

freedom of all people, white and black. I knew as well as I knew anything that the oppressor must be liberated just as surely as the oppressed. A man who takes away another man's freedom is a prisoner of hatred; he is locked behind the bars of prejudice and narrow-mindedness. I am not truly free if I am taking away someone else's freedom, just as surely as I am not free when my freedom is taken away from me. The oppressed and the oppressor alike are robbed of their humanity.[74]

If *ubuntu* is seeking to pursue restorative justice by restoring broken relationships between the victim and the perpetrator, the oppressed and the oppressor, how can this be applied to the theology of lament in the UK context?

Lament as Intercultural Mutuality

African Political Theology, which developed elsewhere on the continent, has a strong contribution to offer in terms of the theology of lament already discussed in chapter one. A prime contribution on lament from an African theological perspective is the work of the Roman Catholic Ugandan theologian Emmanuel Katongole who, in one of his recent books, speaks of the evil and trauma of some of the conflicts in Africa and the need to know how to lament. Katongole unpacks the social dimensions of lament in the midst of suffering, arguing that hope sometimes takes the form of arguing and wrestling with God.[75]

---

[74] Nelson Mandela, *Long Walk to Freedom* (London: Abacus, 1994), p. 751.

[75] Emmanuel Katongole, *Born from Lament: The Theology and Politics of Hope in Africa*

A further reflection on lament is that, is it possible for lament to be construed as a shared pain that can help both Western and Majority World Christians pursue justice together? Black and African theologians have developed lament as a way of resistance, hope, survival and seeking justice, but can lament be offered as intercultural mutuality? What I mean by this is for people of colour and white people to lament together in such a way that we both feel uncomfortable and inconvenienced. In essence, can lament as intercultural mutuality enable us to enter each other's pain and journey together on racial justice concerns? Michael Jagessar, a Black British theologian, talks about intercultural mission as an engagement that should mutually inconvenience us for the sake of justice and inclusion.[76] People of colour are inconvenienced because of legacies of systemic and structural injustices; it is therefore important for white westerners to enter into that pain and be inconvenienced as well. This calls for being ready to be uncomfortable so that we can together pursue justice. We have to both become uncomfortable before we can become comfortable. The implication of this in the UK context is that we need to firstly address the notion that the UK is doing better than America when it comes to race relations. It is often surprising, when having conversations about racial justice, how quickly people point out that we are doing better in the UK compared to America. Please do not get me wrong on this, I am aware that the context in America is very different from the context in the UK. The American context was conquest (Native

---

(Grand Rapids, MI: Eerdmans, 2017). See also Ross, 'Lament and Hope'.

[76] Michael Jagessar, *Ethnicity: The Inclusive Church Resource* (London: Darton, Longman & Todd, 2015).

Americans), slavery, segregation and racial oppression. The UK context is Britain's involvement in the slave trade and colonialism. But the problem is the fact that, whilst America, despite not getting it right, has sought to address the past through ongoing and constant conversations and sometimes owning up to the past, the UK has never really had such conversations or owned up to its involvement in the transatlantic slave trade, colonialism and their legacies. British sensibilities mean that these are issues we do not want to talk about publicly. We are only beginning to talk about it now because George Floyd died on the other side of the Atlantic. But the momentum of that national conversation has now been stalled because of the race report casting doubt on whether institutional racism really exists. The only way we can lament together in the UK is to have these conversations. It will mutually inconvenience us but if we are to pursue justice collectively it is an exercise worth doing. It is the only way we can achieve restorative justice. This is what it means to be the body of Christ so that when one part suffers all suffers (1 Cor. 12:26). Let us lament together, that is, go on a journey of understanding systemic and structural injustices that have defined our world and develop critical questions and actions that can help us address racial justice concerns collaboratively. This is an open invitation to participate in God's mission of reconciliation and bring healing to our society.

In concluding this section, if there is one thing common to all the above-mentioned contextual theologies, it is that they take the suffering of the poor and the oppressed as their hermeneutical lens; therefore, their understanding of discipleship is rooted in Jesus' humility and sacrifice and how that shaped his ministry praxis. The implication of this is that these theologies emphasise that following Jesus entails suffering and loss, and that mission is responding in solidarity with the poor and the oppressed to enable justice. Some of the Majority World Christians who have relocated to Europe and North America through various migratory factors come with this notion and experience of discipleship. Diaspora Christians therefore understand from first-hand experience that discipleship entails different kinds of suffering and demands sacrifice. If the Church is going to do discipleship and mission well in this Corona-climate, we need to grasp Jesus' understanding of suffering and sacrifice. The question is, what is the practical outworking of this for local churches, church networks and mission organisations?

Mission Organisations, Multi-Ethnic Christianity and Racial Justice

In this section, I want to apply some experiences of World Christianity to church networks, mission organisations and theological colleges. These experiences are applying lessons of intercultural mission through multi-ethnic Christianity and racial justice. There are several Western church networks, para-church organisations and mission agencies already doing whole-life discipleship very well, but what I think is missing are the Majority World voices in some of these conversations and organisations. As long as leadership positions in church networks and mission organisations are only filled by Western people, Majority World perspectives and insights will be missing. Some

UK mission agencies and para-church organisations such as the Baptist Missionary Society (BMS), Overseas Missionary Fellowship (OMF) International, Serving in Mission (SIM), Christian Aid and London City Mission have all managed to employ Majority World Christians at a senior staff position.[77] But I am well aware of so many others who have not employed any Majority World Christians, let alone recruited them into senior leadership positions in their organisations, where they can significantly shape mission strategies. There are others who have employed, even in executive leadership roles, but have still failed to engage properly the voices of Majority World theologies or theologians in their discipleship programmes. This is because recruiting one Majority World Christian in a senior leadership position must be viewed as an introduction and not an end strategy, as if one person is enough. In addition, having one Majority World Christian in our senior or executive leadership should never be a substitute for still engaging with Majority World theologies in our discipleship strategies (because, after all, there is a wider range of diversity within Majority World Christian communities).

If church networks and Western mission agencies are going to begin to tackle these issues, then they have to take the challenge

---

[77] Dr. Harvey Kwiyani has just been appointed Global Connections CEO; Dr. Kang-San Tan is the General Director of BMS; Dr. Patrick Fung is the General Director of OMF International; Dr. Joshua Bogunjoko is the International Director of SIM; Amanda Khozi Mukwashi is the CEO of Christian Aid but will be working for the UN from January 2022; Tayo Arikawe is the International Director of Langham Partnership, while Efrem Buckle is the Director of Training and Mentoring at London City Mission. In the past we have also had the late Dr. Joel Edwards lead the Evangelical Alliance, Dr. Rosalee Velosso Ewell lead Redcliffe College and Dr. Wonsuk Ma formerly led the Oxford Centre for Mission Studies.

issued by Churches Together in England on the need for churches to address racial injustices in church life and its structures.[78] This call is not of course limited to the church in England. This will mean church networks and organisations embedding racial justice thinking and action in their processes and structures. Part of this process will include church networks and Western mission organisations de-centring themselves when it comes to racial justice conversations. Too often conversations on racial injustice get hijacked by well-meaning white Christians who are either not comfortable or think they are more informed on the subject. Decentring means you are aware that it is not about you and giving safe spaces to listen to voices people are not accustomed to hearing. It also seems to me that, in the current climate and post-Corona, where resources will be limited, it will become important to consolidate our resources and find pragmatic ways of collaborating together. This will enrich our discipleship activities through the experiences of Majority World Christians, or those of them that now reside in the diaspora. What could be more exciting if we can hear the voices of African theologians, or those of Latin American theologians in our Western apologetics, missional church conversations and discipleship training? After all, these are the regions of the world where Christianity is growing and thriving despite the fact there is much suffering, so surely we have something to learn from these contexts.

---

[78] Churches Together in England, 'CTE Presidents call all churches to address racial injustice in church life and wider society',
https://cte.org.uk/Articles/584547/Home/News/Latest_news/CTE_Presidents_cal l.aspx (accessed 28 July 2020).

If the concerns of racial justice are an important part of building strategic collaboration with Christians from the Majority World, how can church networks, Western mission agencies and theological colleges achieve this? A good place to start on this journey is to understand God's vision of a multi-ethnic kingdom. John in the Book of Revelation gives us a glimpse of this vision when he describes the liturgy sung in heaven by the four living creatures and the twenty-four elders: 'They sing a new song: you are worthy to take the scroll and to open its seals, for you were slaughtered and by your blood you ransomed for God saints from every tribe and language and people and nation; you have made them to be kingdom and priests serving our God, and they will reign on earth' (Rev. 5:9-10, *NRSV*). This heavenly liturgy describes God's kingdom in terms of tribes, languages, peoples and nations, signifying that his kingdom was never meant to be about one tribe, language, people or nation. In essence, God's kingdom is not designed to be mono-ethnic or monocultural but is multi-ethnic in its DNA. I also find it fascinating that the heavenly liturgy did not blur the distinctions of the tribes, the languages, the peoples and the nations, meaning God is not colour blind! God is not colour blind because he created people of colour in the first place. God created one human race, but that humanity is expressed in different physical features, skin pigmentations, geographic locations, cultures and histories. Paul puts it this way: 'From one man he made all the nations, that they should inhabit the whole earth; and he marked out their appointed times in history and the boundaries of their land' (Acts 17:26, *NIV*). Paul seems to be suggesting that God created one human race but puts us in different geographic locations on his earth for a reason.

I find it liberating that God created one human race in his image, but yet allowed humanity to be expressed in different geographic locations. God's idea of one human race in his image, though expressed in different parts of the world, is also what constituted the central worship of the Lamb by a great multitude drawn from every tribe, people and language in John's vision in Revelation (Rev. 7:9-10). In essence, God created us differently but, because we are one humanity fashioned in his image, he wants us to worship him together. This reflects the nature of the Godhead itself, which is three distinct persons but one in essence. This is the theology that underpins a biblical unity in diversity that is expressed in God's multi-ethnic kingdom. But the idea of one human race has, however, been distorted and corrupted through history, particularly the history of navigation, European expansion and empire. As Europeans began to travel the world as merchants, navigators and explorers they came in contact with people who looked different from them. The question of how you define and relate to the other became an issue. This led to the idea of different races and racial categorisation that affirms the superiority of Caucasians and dehumanises Africans, Asians and indigenous people in the Americas and elsewhere. The consequence was a racial ideology which manifested in the history of the slave trade, colonialism, indentured servitude and neo-colonialism. How can the Church get back to God's vision of a multi-ethnic kingdom or, more specifically, how can the UK church express this vision in our church networks, mission agencies and theological colleges?

Firstly, in order for our churches, mission agencies and theological colleges to become places where God's multi-ethnic kingdom is expressed, we have to be intentional in our thinking, strategies and action. People often desire and want a multicultural or multi-ethnic church, college or organisation, but are not prepared to do the hard work that it requires. Has your board of directors or trustees intentionally sought to have on the team people of Asian, African or Latin American background? Does your five-year strategy plan intentionally include engaging Majority World Christians and churches? Does your national leadership team only have PLUs (People Like Us)? The early church was intentional in nominating and appointing Grecian Jews when they felt marginalised by the Hebraic Jews. A study of the names of the seven leaders (deacons) selected demonstrates this intentionality (see Acts 6:1-7).

Secondly, we need to create safe spaces in our church streams, mission agencies and theological colleges to have conversations about race and racism. Churches too many times shy away from having these conversations because it makes people feel uncomfortable. If we are going to move forward, we need to have these conversations and the murder of George Floyd has certainly given us the framework for us to have these conversations. Can our church meetings or board meetings be dedicated to talk about the issue of race and racism? Do our theological colleges have compulsory modules on Black Theology, African Theology and post-colonial theologies? Can our national conferences begin to address some of these issues as the main theme rather than relegating it to a seminar or track focusing on the subject?

Thirdly, our churches, mission organisations and theological colleges need to listen to Majority World voices (Africa, Asia, the Caribbean and Latin America). This is partly to understand the pain and hurt that Majority World Christians have been carrying or have internalised as a result of not being heard. In a church context that already has an ethnically diverse congregation, it becomes imperative to listen to those marginal voices who are not normally heard or promoted. Pastors, principals and CEOs need to remember that this is also a pastoral issue because, as those people begin to share, issues they have internalised will surface. Therefore, before creating those safe spaces to listen, ask yourself whether your church or organisation has the appropriate level of support put in place for those people. This process could also bring healing to the whole church or mission organisation if it is handled with transparency and honesty. In the case of theological colleges, what sort of theological textbooks do we recommend as essential reading on our reading list? It is not enough to have Majority World guest speakers teaching the occasional Diaspora Missiology or World Christianity module. Efforts must be made to recruit as part of the teaching faculty Majority World Christians. This will mean looking critically at our recruitment and employment processes. This also applies to mission agencies and para-church organisations.

Lastly, our churches and organisations need to learn the history of racism. Part of that will mean putting into perspective the history of the modern missionary movement in the light of its collusion with colonialism. A re-orientation of history is also needed so that we not only see William Wilberforce as the champion of freedom, but the likes of ex-slaves such as Olaudah

Equiano (1745–1797) and Ottobah Cugoano (1757–1791), who were part of the abolitionist movement. Part of our learning will also include knowing how European history has created people we now call African Americans, African Caribbeans, Africans and Black British. Our journey towards a multi-ethnic congregation, mission agency or college requires understanding white hegemony (supremacy), and one way of doing that is to learn about black history.

A further thought is, what perspectives can Western apologetics, the missional church movement and the whole-life discipleship movement learn from Majority World theologians that can reinvigorate our missiology? We have seen a glimpse of this reimagining through the works of Western theologians and missionaries who spent many years serving in the Majority World before relocating back to the West with fresh missional perspectives. An example is Lesslie Newbigin (1909–1998), who served as a missionary in India for several years, returning to the UK with a new lens to critique the Enlightenment-dominated approach to mission. Newbigin provides a brilliant analysis of contemporary culture in its secular, humanist and pluralistic characteristics and then offers ways of how Western Christians can confidently affirm their faith in such contexts.[79] It is his work that inspires the genesis of the missional church conversations from the early 1980s on both sides of the Atlantic.

Another is Harold W. Turner, a fine theologian from New Zealand (1911–2002), who served as a missionary scholar in Sierra Leone before returning to the UK with new insights on reading the

---

[79] Lesslie Newbigin, *The Gospel in a Pluralist Society* (London: SPCK, 1989).

European culture and how the gospel can penetrate the European worldview. While he is best known for creating and documenting what is referred to as New Religious Movements (NRM), his three levels of holistic mission engagement, personal, social and cultural, provide a fresh critique of how we should engage the worldviews of the European context.[80]

A last example is Andrew Walls (1928–2021), who served as a colleague of Harold Turner in Sierra Leone before returning to Scotland and England. Andrew Walls' pioneering insight on the shift of Christianity to the southern hemisphere is hugely significant for what is referred to as Diaspora Missiology.[81] The point is this: these three white men, who have contributed to our understanding of the West as a new mission field with the need to engage it afresh, all developed their thinking in the laboratories of the Majority World context. They all had the benefit of stepping outside Western culture and, in that, were able to critique it with an outsider's perspective. The inference then is, if Western missiology has been enriched by Western theologians who have interacted with the Majority World context and theologies, how much more enriched will Western apologetics, missional church conversations and whole-life discipleship training be if they engage meaningfully with Majority World Christians and their theologies? This will of course include voices of women and men from these contexts and not just men!

---

[80] Harold Turner, 'Deep Mission to Deep Culture' in John Flett (ed.), *Collision Crossroads: The Intersection of Modern Western Culture with the Christian Gospel* (Auckland: Deep Sight Publishing, 1998), pp. 14-33.

[81] Andrew Walls, *Crossing Cultural Frontiers: Studies in the History of World Christianity* (Maryknoll, NY: Orbis Books, 2017).

Questions for Individual Reflection
or Group Discussions

- What can Western Christians learn about the theology of suffering from Majority World Christians?
- How can post-colonial contextual theologies inform Western models of discipleship?
- How do some Majority World cultures and worldviews enhance whole-life discipleship?
- Discuss why suffering and discipleship are going to be important for the pandemic and post-pandemic context?
- How is your church or organisation engaging voices from the Majority World?

Chapter Four
Concluding Reflections:
Post-Covid-19 Church

This book has been about exploring discipleship and suffering and how Western discipleship models need to be reconfigured through the lens of racial justice. This is because the pandemic context has exposed social justice issues that current discipleship models have struggled to engage with properly in the past. I have proposed that Western whole-life discipleship models can be enriched with the Jubilee theological framework that emphasises covenant community, economic justice and creation care.

It is very clear from the impact of the pandemic on humanity that it has stirred big questions such as, what is the meaning of life? Is there a purpose to suffering and pain? If God exists, why does he allow so much suffering? What makes us human? I have provided preliminary answers to some of these questions, whilst some other questions have been left unanswered to provoke further thoughts and conversations. But how the Church seeks to respond to these questions will determine its future relevance and shape its mission. I am not sure if we can even begin to speak of post-Covid-19 yet because we are still living through the pandemic and its impact on our world, but I live in hope, and therefore offer some reflections for a post-pandemic context. Will the post-Covid-19 Church need to be equipped with apologetics in order to engage people at an intellectual level? While I think this is going to be particularly important, the Church will also need an emotional strategy and response by grieving with people together. This will require the Church to be equipped with the theology of suffering and lament discussed in chapters one and three that can enable us to create safe spaces for people to grieve and lament. Lament can also be a powerful tool for social justice and therefore very important in our discipleship models. There are Christian organisations already journeying with people using lament. Care for the Family and Safe Families are two Christian organisations who are already engaging families and communities in this area of work. Another is the Racial Justice Advocacy Forum, which is using lament as a tool to pursue what can be best described as reparative justice.

The post-Covid-19 Church must also come to terms with our ecological responsibility. The whole Church must be geared for this rather than leaving the agenda to some section of the Church. If the statistics coming from the Center for the Study of Global Christianity are right that say that the continent of Africa now has the highest number of Christians in the world,[82] it will then become increasingly important that African Christianity, in all its myriad expressions and its diaspora constituency, engage fully with the issues of environmental justice. Some expressions of African Christianity on the continent are beginning to address

---

[82] Center for the Study of Global Christianity, Gordon-Conwell Theological Seminary, *Christianity in its Global Context 1970–2020: Society, Religion, and Mission* (2013), pp. 6-7.

these issues through African Public Theology.[83] However, we need a wider participation and especially that of African churches in the diaspora. Working groups, such as the efforts of Christian Aid and some key Black Majority Church leaders, theologians and activists will become significant for the future.

The significance of this working group is that it approaches the issues of climate justice through the perspective of racial justice. It explores the intersectionality of climate justice and racial justice historically and its ongoing legacies of disproportional ecological impact on people from the Majority World. One methodology of doing this is through promoting the Brown Agenda alongside the Green Agenda. The Green Agenda, focusing on conservation and preservation of plants and animals, has shaped the global narrative and discourse on climate change. Therefore the need to promote the Brown Agenda, which looks at the impact and connection of ecological degradation and exploitative economies on people of colour. Giving due emphasis to the Brown Agenda alongside the Green Agenda could create a balance of what some African theologians are referring to as the Olive Agenda.[84] That is, a holistic approach to climate justice, exploring the impact of ecological degradation on people of colour, plants and animals. It considers the entire ecosystem and biodiversity of our world.

The identity question that the Black Lives Matter movement raises will continue to be of importance, especially in the UK with the commissioned report on Race and Ethnic Disparities

---

[83] Sunday Bobai Agang, Dion A. Forster and H. Jurgens Hendriks (eds), *African Public Theology* (Plateau State, Nigeria: Hippo Books, 2020).

[84] Agang et al., *African Public Theology*.

conclusions that there is anecdotal evidence for institutional racism or that there is only anecdotal evidence for institutional racism. But what will be crucial is how society, and in particular how the UK church, engages with this issue. For example, if the UK church chooses to intentionally go on a journey and engage with this identity issue, then we could have an authentic intercultural church unity develop. But if there is a refusal to engage genuinely, this could potentially lead to church segregation, where we have white churches, organisations and agencies doing their own thing without any reference to black churches and organisations. Some might say that already describes our current engagement, but this could get even worse and more polarised. There are, however, signs in the UK church that conversations are beginning to happen regarding racial justice issues. Three examples are, firstly, the Church of England report *From Lament to Action*. A second is the panel conversations on racial justice organised by Fresh Streams (a Baptist Charismatic network) in their annual leadership conference in 2021. A third is the Churches Charter for Racial Justice, created by some senior church leaders in Birmingham to address issues of racial injustice in church and society. These are at early stages, and it is hoped that they will not be tokenistic or just an exercise to tick a diversity box, but that they will develop to fruitful conversations.

How can the Church discern the prophetic at this critical time in human history? What impact does post-Covid-19 have on the future of mission? The pandemic has uncovered and continues to expose the social inequality issues that have plagued our world. One such is that, while the virus affects everyone irrespective of colour, class, age or gender, it has become very clear that it disproportionally impacts poorer people and people of colour. This racial inequality issue has also been amplified as a direct result of the murder of George Floyd. Therefore, the Church is now in a Cornelius moment so that, just as Peter was convicted by God realising that the new body of believers can not only be Jewish Christians, but that Greek Christians are an essential part of that body, Western Christianity can no longer operate on the false dichotomy of mission and racial justice. We need a vision of a just society post-pandemic that can address racial inequalities and empower people of colour to attain human flourishing.

If the Western church, in all its diverse expressions, is going to be an agent of social change, speaking truth to power, then it has to do something it is not very good at; that is, listen to Majority World voices on the issues of discipleship and suffering. Part of that will mean Western evangelical Christians will have to take the issues of racial justice as an essential category of their missiology. Mission studies will have to be reconfigured in the light of racial justice. I am not trying to stereotype all Western evangelical Christians because, firstly, the evangelical constituency is broad and very diverse.[85] Secondly, there are definitely some Western evangelicals who are seriously engaging and championing racial justice causes, but the question is, why has it not become the normal practice? To put the question another way, why are racial justice issues not an important part

---

[85] Western evangelicals are a broad spectrum covering a range of church traditions, countries and movements. These include reformed, charismatics, conservative, progressives, ecumenicals and radicals. These tags or labels are not exhaustive, but they are a start.

of Western evangelical mission theology? I have provided some preliminary answers to these questions in chapter one of this book.

But here are some further reflections. One reason is that racial justice conversations are very uncomfortable for some Western evangelicals because of white guilt and shame. This is where understanding lament as intercultural mutuality discussed in chapter three, that inconveniences us together, is significant. Another reason which other people have commented on is white privilege,[86] which becomes a blind spot obscuring racial justice concerns. Lastly is perhaps how some Western evangelicals read and interpret the biblical texts and do theology. If evangelical charismatics sometimes spiritualise the scriptures so that there is more emphasis on growing in discipleship through the Holy Spirit and our giftings, some reformed evangelicals move in the other direction of growing in discipleship through the word, that is, biblical exposition. These are good and needed emphases, but what is sometimes missing is a post-colonial reading of scriptures that situates the text in colonial thinking, that is, relating the biblical text to colonial history because of similarity of context. This means it is possible to talk about God seeing Moses' staff as a gift of the Spirit but not dwell on the slavery context of the children of Israel and how that resonates today with the experiences of so many people from the Majority World. It is possible to expound on the book of Daniel but miss the crucial

---

[86] For example, Chine McDonald, *God is Not a White Man*. Also Anthony Reddie and Ravelle-Sadé Fairman's podcast on 'White Supremacy and Black Suffering', *Nomad*, 23 June 2020, https://www.nomadpodcast.co.uk/anthony-reddie-ravelle-sade-fairman-white-supremacy-and-black-suffering-n226/ (accessed 5 May 2021).

points that nevertheless, Daniel and the three Hebrew children were colonised by the Babylonians and the implication of that for a decolonised thinking in today's context.

There is the need for some Western evangelicals to decolonise their mission theology and a good place to start is to re-examine what is taught at our theological institutions. As someone who lectures and teaches in various theological institutions in the UK, I see some good signs, but more work needs to be done. This work needs to be done by introducing the history of slavery and colonialism into our history of mission curriculum or modules. Another area that needs work is allowing Africans, Asians, African Caribbeans and Latin Americans to not only come in and speak on Diaspora Mission, as if that is all we can offer, but to teach biblical studies and systematic theology. The issue is sometimes raised of not knowing qualified biblical scholars who are of the Majority World who can teach these subjects. The problem sometimes is our limited network, which constantly draws in people from the same pool; let us widen our networks so that we can connect beyond people like us! (PLUs).

Another area that needs work in terms of decolonising our mission theology is, instead of constantly inviting Africans or Asians to come in occasionally to teach on multi-ethnic churches, why not employ them as part-time staff or associate tutors? I am aware that some theological colleges in the UK have made some progress on this front, but if Western evangelicals are going to begin to engage broadly with the concerns of racial justice, then we have to seriously think of a higher percentage of employment and staffing of Majority World Christians at our theological colleges to shift the balance.

Western theological colleges are where the gatekeepers are trained; if the gatekeepers are not well equipped to discern racial justice matters in their locality, then racial injustice will happen under their leadership, and they will not even recognise it. It is time to shift our theological colleges in the direction of racial justice, and to do this we have to decolonise our curriculum.

Another implication of this listening exercise is that it will allow for a further deepening of the decolonising process of our mission practices from the Western Christendom model that has had its hold for a long time on the mission of the Church. It is becoming clear that the Church cannot minister effectively post-Covid-19 if it does not understand suffering and loss. While everyone suffers, the suffering that has shaped Majority World Christians and therefore their theologies is one area the Western church will have to pay attention to for its future mission. I have argued in this book that a good place to start is to understand Jesus' model of discipleship rooted in suffering and sacrifice.

Jesus' idea of suffering and sacrifice as hallmarks of discipleship is going to be very important for the mission of the Church for a post-pandemic world of ongoing grief, loss and trauma. As articulated in this book, I have suggested that the UK church can learn from the experiences of Majority World Christians in understanding this model of discipleship rooted in liminality and humility. For this to happen, we need a collaboration that engages the voices of Majority World theologians in the Western whole-life discipleship, missional church conversations and apologetics movement. This will require strategic collaboration that employs a racial justice rationale in its procedures and dealings. This will also require intercultural translators who can oscillate between different communities to usher in God's kingdom purposes.

In concluding, I am aware that several mission organisations, church networks and theological institutions are researching and writing about how the Church can engage in mission in this pandemic and post-pandemic context; therefore, this book is not offered as the last word on the subject but as a contribution to the ongoing dialogue.

Questions for Individual Reflection
or Group Discussions

- I have used the words 'post-Covid-19' in this last chapter: are we still in the pandemic or post-pandemic, and also, what are your hopes and aspirations for the future?
- In your own opinion, what do you think the post-Covid-19 church is going to look like?
- What are the things you think will be essential for a post-Covid-19 church?
- What role will racial justice matters play in the future of the church?
- What are you or your church, mission organisation, theological college (or workplace) discerning for the future?

Bibliography

Agang, Sunday Bobai, Dion A. Forster and H. Jurgens Hendriks, Eds. *African Public Theology*. Plateau State, Nigeria: Hippo Books, 2020.

Augustine, *City of God*. Trans. Henry Bettenson. London: Penguin Books, 2003.

Beckford, Robert. 'From Maintenance to Mission: Resisting the Bewitchment of Colonial Christianity'. In *Challenges of Black Pentecostal Leadership in the 21st Century*. Ed. Phyllis Thompson. London: SPCK, 2013, 32-51.

Beckford, Robert. *Jesus is Dread: Black Theology and Black Culture in Britain*. London: Darton, Longman & Todd, 1998.

Beckford, Robert. *Dread and Pentecostal: A Political Theology for the Black Church in Britain*. London: SPCK, 2000.

Blasu, Ebenezer Yaw. 'The Invisible Global War: An African "Theocological" Assessment of Responses to Covid-19'. *Evangelical Review of Theology* 44:4 (2020), 302-312.

Bosch, David. *Transforming Mission: Paradigm Shifts in Theology of Mission* (20th Anniversary Edition). Maryknoll, NY: Orbis Books, 2014.

Cameron, Helen and Catherine Duce. *Researching Practice in Ministry and Mission: A Companion*. London: SCM Press, 2013.

Center for the Study of Global Christianity, Gordon-Conwell Theological Seminary. *Christianity in its Global Context 1970–2020: Society, Religion, and Mission*. 2013.

Christian Aid. *A Prophetic Journey Towards Climate Justice: Terms of Reference of the Working Group with Black Majority Churches*. PowerPoint document, 2020.

Cone, James H. *A Black Theology of Liberation* (20th Anniversary Edition). Maryknoll, NY: Orbis Books, 2004.

Ertan, Deniz, Wissam El-Hage, Sarah Thierrée, Hervé Javelot and Coraline Hingray. 'COVID-19: Urgency for distancing from domestic violence'. *European Journal of Psychotraumatology* 11:1 (2020).

Escobar, Samuel. *The New Global Mission: The Gospel from Everywhere to Everyone*. Downers Grove, IL: IVP Academic, 2003.

Foxe, John and M. Hobart Seymour. *The Acts and Monuments of the Church: Containing the History and Sufferings of the Martyrs*, Part 1. London: Charter House, 1838.

Green, Mark. *Thank God it's Monday: Ministry in the Workplace*. Bletchley: Scripture Union, 2001.

Green, Mark. *Fruitfulness on the Frontline: Making a Difference Where You Are*. Nottingham: IVP, 2014.

Guder, Darrell. L., Ed. *Missional Church: A Vision for the Sending of the Church in North America*. Grand Rapids, MI: Eerdmans, 1998.

Gutiérrez, Gustavo. *A Theology of Liberation*. London: SCM Press, 1974.

Hanciles, Jehu. *Beyond Christendom: Globalization, African Migration, and the Tranformation of the West*. Maryknoll, NY: Orbis Books, 2008.

Isaac, Les. *Relevant Church: A God-Given Goal*. London: Ascension Trust, 2004.

Jagessar, Michael. *Ethnicity: The Inclusive Church Resource*. London: Darton, Longman & Todd, 2015.

Katongole, Emmanuel. *Born from Lament: The Theology and Politics of Hope in Africa*. Grand Rapids, MI: Eerdmans, 2017.

Kumar, Anant. 'COVID-19 and Domestic Violence: A Possible Public Health Crisis'. *Journal of Health Management* 22:2 (2020), 192-196.

Lennox, John. *Where is God in a Coronavirus World?* Epson: Good Books Company, 2020.

Lindsay, Ben. *We Need To Talk About Race: Understanding the Black Experience in White Majority Churches*. London: SPCK, 2019.

Louth, Andrew, Ed. *Eusebius: The History of the Church*. Trans. G.A. Williamson. Harmondsworth: Penguin Books, 1965.

Mandela, Nelson. *Long Walk to Freedom*. London: Abacus, 1994.

Mandryk, Jason. *Global Transmission, Global Mission: The Impact and Implications of the COVID-19 Pandemic*. Manchester: Operation World, 2020.

McDonald, Chine. *God is Not a White Man: And Other Revelations*. London: Hodder & Stoughton, 2021.

Moltmann, Jürgen. *The Crucified God*. London: SCM Press, 1974.

Moore, Basil, Ed. *Black Theology: South African Voice*. London: C. Hurst & Company, 1973.

Moynagh Michael. *Emergingchurch.intro*. Oxford: Monarch Books, 2004.

Moynagh Michael. *Church for Every Context: An Introduction to Theology and Practice*. London: SCM Press, 2012.

Moynagh Michael. *Church in Life: Innovations, Mission and Ecclesiology*. London: SCM Press, 2017.

Niebuhr, Richard. *Christ and Culture*. New York: Harper and Row, 1951.

Newbigin, Lesslie. *The Gospel in a Pluralist Society*. London: SPCK, 1989.

Padilla, René. *Mission Between the Times*. Carlisle: Langham Monographs, 2010.

Parratt, John. *Reinventing Christianity: African Theology Today*. Cambridge: Eerdmans, 1995.

Peterman, Amber, Alina Potts, Megan O' Donnell, Kelly Thompson, Niyati Shah, Sabine Oertelt-Prigione, and Nicole van Gelder. *Pandemics and Violence against Women and Children*. Center for Global Development, working paper 528, 2020.

Stott, John. *Issues Facing Christians Today*. London: HarperCollins, 1984.

Stroope, Michael. *Transcending Mission: The Eclipse of a Modern Tradition*. London: Apollos, 2017.

Slee, Nicola. *Sabbath: The Hidden Heartbeat of our Lives*. London: Darton, Longman & Todd, 2019.

Tidball, Derek. *Who are the Evangelicals? Tracing the Roots of the Modern Day Movement*. London: HarperCollins, 1994.

Tomlinson, Dave. *The Post-Evangelical*. London: SPCK, 1995.

Turner, Harold. 'Deep Mission to Deep Culture'. In *Collision Crossroads: The Intersection of Modern Western Culture with the Christian Gospel*, Ed. John Flett. Auckland: Deep Sight Publishing, 1998, 14-33.

Tutu, Desmond. *No Future Without Forgiveness.* London: Random House, 1999.

Walls, Andrew. *Crossing Cultural Frontiers: Studies in the History of World Christianity.* Maryknoll, NY: Orbis Books, 2017.

Ware, Joe and Chine McDonald. *Black Lives Matter Everywhere: A Study of Public Attitudes Towards Race and Climate Change.* London: Christian Aid, 2020.

Wurmbrand, Richard. *Tortured for Christ.* London: Hodder & Stoughton, 2004 (1940).

Yamauchi, Edwin. *The World of the First Christians.* Tring: Lion Publishing, 1981.

Online Sources

Accad, Martin. 'Theological Education as Formation for Prophetic Ministry'. Arab Baptist Theological Seminary, 1 August 2019. https://abtslebanon.org/2019/08/01/theological-education-as-formation-for-prophetic-ministry-2/ (Accessed 27 December 2020).

Amos, Jonathan. BBC News, 27 March 2020. 'Coronavirus: Lockdown continues to suppress European pollution'. https://www.bbc.co.uk/news/science-environment-52065140 (Accessed 6 May 2020).

Ascension Trust. https://www.ascensiontrust.org.uk/ (Accessed 1 October 2020).

BBC News, 23 September 2020. 'Climate Movement does not represent me'. https://www.bbc.co.uk/news/av/uk-54209707 (Accessed 1 October 2020).

BBC News, 24 January 2020. 'Vanessa Nakate: Climate activist hits out at "racist" photo crop'. https://www.bbc.co.uk/news/world-africa-51242972 (Accessed 1 October 2020).

Beckford, Robert. 'Better Must Come! Black Pentecostals, the Pandemic and the future of Christianity'. https://vimeo.com/414095431 (Accessed 18 May 2020).

Being Human Project. https://www.eauk.org/what-we-do/initiatives/being-human (Accessed 31 December 2020).

Care for the Family. https://www.careforthefamily.org.uk/Family+life/bereavement-support (Accessed 1 October 2020).

Commission on Race and Ethnic Disparities. https://www.gov.uk/government/publications/the-report-of-the-commission-on-race-and-ethnic-disparities (Accessed 2 April 2021).

Commission on Race and Ethnic Disparities. Statement on the report published 31 March 2021. https://www.gov.uk/government/news/the-commission-on-race-and-ethnic-disparities-statement (Accessed 4 April 2021).

Church of England, *From Lament to Action: The Report of the Archbishop's Anti-racism Taskforce*. https://www.churchofengland.org/sites/default/files/2021-04/FromLamentToAction-report.pdf (Accessed 26 April 2021).

Churches Together in England. *Pentecostal and Charismatic Churches and COVID-19*. https://cte.org.uk/Articles/579120/Home/Coronavirus/Pentecostal_and_Charismatic.aspx (Accessed 1 June 2020).

Churches Together in England. 'Presidents call all churches to address racial injustice in church life and wider society'. https://cte.org.uk/Articles/584547/Home/News/Latest_news/CTE_Presidents_call.aspx (Accessed 28 July 2020).

Evangelical Alliance. *Changing Church: Autumn Survey Executive Summary*. https://www.eauk.org/assets/files/downloads/Changing-Church-autumn-survey-executive-summary.pdf (Accessed 4 November 2020).

Faith and Leadership. 'Maggie Barankitse: Love made me an inventor'. https://www.youtube.com/watch?v=PWSxAA4nOg0 (Accessed 4 May 2021).

Geddes, Linda. *The Guardian*, 16 January 2021. 'Covid vaccine: 72% of black people unlikely to have jab, UK survey finds'. https://www.theguardian.com/world/2021/jan/16/covid-vaccine-black-people-unlikely-covid-jab-uk?CMP=Share_iOSApp_Other (Accessed 17 January 2021).

Intergovernmental Panel on Climate Change (IPCC). Sixth Assessment Report. https://www.ipcc.ch/assessment-report/ar6/ (Accessed 13 August 2021).

ITV News, 13 May 2020. 'Discrimination on frontline of Coronavirus outbreak may be factor in disproportionate BAME deaths among NHS staff'. https://www.itv.com/news/2020-05-13/discrimination-frontline-coronavirus-covid19-black-minority-ethnic-bame-deaths-nhs-racism/ (Accessed 14 May 2020).

Jamir, Shiluinla. 'Embracing God's Beloved Community: Rethinking Mission in Asia during COVID-19 and Beyond'. Asia CMS, 2020. https://www.asiacms.net/news/asiacms-proudly-presents-a-new-book-on-rethinking-mission-in-asia-during-covid-19-and-beyond/ (Accessed 13 February 2021).

Kintsugi Hope. https://www.kintsugihope.com/vision (Accessed 28 September 2020).

Kwiyani, Harvey. 'Mission After George Floyd: On White Supremacy, Colonialism and World Christianity'. *Journal of Theology and Mission* 36:2 (2020). https://churchmissionsociety.org/resources/mission-after-george-floyd-on-white-supremacy-colonialism-and-world-christianity-harvey-kwiyani-anvil-vol-36-issue-3/ (Accessed 29 April 2021).

Latham, Steve. 'Corona-theology'. Jeremiad Essays blog, 23 March 2020. http://jeremiadstevelatham.blogspot.com/2020/03/corona-theology.html (Accessed 1 May 2020).

Messy Church. 'What Messy Church is and isn't'. https://www.messychurch.org.uk/what-messy-church-and-isnt (Accessed 6 May 2020).

Mormina, Maru and Ifeanyi Nsofor, 'What developing countries can teach rich countries about how to respond to a pandemic'. *The Conversation*, 15 October 2020. https://theconversation.com/what-developing-countries-can-teach-rich-countries-about-how-to-respond-to-a-pandemic-146784 (Accessed 25 October 2020).

Needham, Oliver. 'A Quarter of UK Adults engage in Religious Services Online during Lockdown'. Oliver Needham blog, 3 May 2020. https://oliverneedham.co.uk/blog/2020/05/a-quarter-of-uk-adults-engage-with-religious-services-online-during-lockdown/ (Accessed 4 May 2020).

NHS Vaccine Facts. 'I had the vaccine because I want to be there for my sons'. https://www.nhsvaccinefacts.com/stories/i-had-the-vaccine-for-my-sons (Accessed 28 May 2021).

Olofinjana, Israel. 'Coronavirus: A New Paradigm for Discipleship and Mission'. Hope 15:13, 6 May 2020. https://hope1513.com/2020/05/06/coronavirus-a-new-paradigm-for-discipleship-and-mission-by-rev-israel-oluwole-olofinjana/ (Accessed April 2020).

Olofinjana, Israel. 'Decolonising Mission: Learning from the Majority World Template of Suffering and Sacrifice'. *Lausanne Global Analysis* 9:5 (September 2020). https://lausanne.org/lga-04/decolonizing-mission (Accessed 15 September 2020).

Olofinjana, Israel. 'Discerning the Prophetic: Perspective of Majority World Theologies on Suffering and Sacrifice'. *Baptist Together Magazine*. https://www.baptist.org.uk/Articles/587272/Discerning_the_prophetic.aspx (Accessed 15 September 2020).

Reddie, Anthony and Ravelle-Sadé Fairman. 'White Supremacy and Black Suffering'. *Nomad*, 23 June 2020. https://www.nomadpodcast.co.uk/anthony-reddie-ravelle-sade-fairman-white-supremacy-and-black-suffering-n226/ (Accessed 5 May 2021).

Rievan, Kirst. 'In a Pandemic, Should Missionaries Leave or Stay? A Mental Model for the Missiology of Risk'. *Lausanne Global Analysis* 9:4 (July 2020). https://lausanne.org/content/lga/2020-07/in-a-pandemic-should-missionaries-leave-or-stay (Accessed 23 August 2020).

Ross, Cathy. 'Lament and Hope'. *ANVIL: Journal of Theology and Mission* 34:1 (2018). https://churchmissionsociety.org/resources/lament-and-hope-cathy-ross-anvil-vol-34-issue-1/ (Accessed 6 May 2020).

UK African COVID-19 Experience. http://www.ukafricancovidexp.org/ (Accessed 1 October 2020).

Wooden, Cindy. *Crux*, 20 March 2020. 'If you can't go to confession, take your sorrow directly to God, says Pope'. https://cruxnow.com/vatican/2020/03/if-you-cant-go-to-confession-take-your-sorrow-directly-to-god-pope-says/ (Accessed 29 September 2020).

Recommended Resources for Further Studies

Racial Justice

BBC Panorama. *Is the Church Racist?* 19 April 2021.

Coleman, Kate. 'Accepting Ethnic Diversity and Difference'. Missio Nexus, 2020. https://missionexus.org/accepting-ethnic-diversity-and-difference/ (Accessed April 2021).

Eddo-Lodge, Reni. *Why I'm No Longer Talking to White People About Race.* London: Bloomsbury Publishing, 2018.

McCaulley, Esau. *Reading While Black: African American Biblical Interpretation as an Exercise in Hope.* Downers Grove, IL: IVP Academic, 2020.

Parekh, Bhikhu. *The Future of Multi-Ethnic Britain: Report of the Commission on the Future of Multi-Ethnic Britain.* London: Profile Books, 2000.

Reddie, Anthony. *Is God Colour-Blind? Insights from Black Theology for Christian Faith and Ministry.* London: SPCK, 2020.

Reddie, Anthony. *Theologising Brexit: A Liberationist and Postcolonial Critique.* Abingdon: Routledge, 2019.

Church Unity

Alded, Joe. *Respect: Understanding Caribbean British Christianity.* Peterborough: Epworth Press, 2005.

Clifford, Steve. *One: Unity in Diversity – A Personal Journey.* Oxford: Monarch Books, 2017.

Edwards, Joel. *Lord, Make Us One – But Not All the Same!* London: Hodder & Stoughton, 1999.

Olofinjana, Israel. *Partnership in Mission: A Black Majority Church Perspective on Mission and Church Unity.* Watford: Instant Apostle, 2015.

Mission

Adeney, Francis S. *Women and Christian Mission: Ways of Knowing and Doing Theology.* Eugene, OR: Cascade Books, 2015.

Botha, Nico A. and Eugene Baron. *Majority World Perspectives on Christian Mission.* South Africa: Kreativ, 2020.

Cueva, Samuel. *Mission Partnership in Creative Tension*. Carlisle: Langham Monographs, 2015.

Dowsett, Rose, Ed. *Global Mission: Reflections and Case Studies in Local Theology for the Whole Church (Globalization of Mission)*. Pasadena, CA: William Carey Library, 2011.

Kumbi, Hirpo. *Mission and Movement: A Study of Ethiopian and Eritrean Evangelical Churches in the UK*. Watford: Instant Apostle, 2018.

Kwiyani, Harvey. *Sent Forth: African Missionary Work in the West*. Maryknoll, NY: Orbis Books, 2014.

Mohammed, Arif, Ram Gidoomal, Robin Thompson and Raju Abraham. *Diaspora Mission: The Story of South Asian Concern*. London: South Asian Concern, 2014.

Olofinjana, Israel. *World Christianity in Western Europe: Diasporic Identities, Narratives and Missiology*. Oxford: Regnum Publishing, 2020.

Olofinjana, Israel. *Reverse in Ministry and Missions: Africans in the Dark Continent of Europe*. Milton Keynes: Author House, 2010.

Reifsnider, Usha. *Cross-cultural Mission in Relation to Migrants*. Spring Harvest, 2020. https://www.youtube.com/watch?v=FmVBq3tEMe4 (Accessed April 2021).

Robert, Dana L. *Gospel Bearers, Gender Barriers: Missionary Women in the Twentieth Century*. Maryknoll, NY: Orbis Books, 2002.

Ross, Cathy and Stephen Bevans, Eds. *Mission on the Road to Emmaus: Constants, Context, and Prophetic Dialogue*. Maryknoll, NYk: Orbis Books, 2015.

Walls, Andrew. *The Missionary Movement in Christian History: Studies in the Transmission of Faith*. Edinburgh: T&T Clark, 1996.

Walls, Andrew. *The Cross-Cultural Process in Christian History*. Edinburgh: T&T Clark, 2002.

Intercultural Churches (Multicultural and Multi-Ethnic Churches and Ministries)

Kwiyani, Harvey. *Multicultural Kingdom: Ethnic Diversity, Mission and the Church*. London: SCM Press, 2020.

Mukwashi, Amanda Khozi. *But Where Are You Really From? On Identity, Humanhood and Hope*. London: SPCK, 2020.

Olofinjana, Israel. *Turning the Tables on Mission: Stories of Christians from the Global South in the UK*. Watford: Instant Apostle, 2013.

Otaigbe, Osoba. *Building Cultural Intelligence in Church and Ministry*. Milton Keynes: Author House, 2016.

Patten, Malcolm. *Leading a Multicultural Church*. London: SPCK, 2016.

Prentis, Sharon. *Every Tribe: Stories of Diverse Saints Serving a Diverse World*. London: SPCK, 2019.

Reddie, Anthony, Seidel Abel-Boarneges, Pam Searle. *Intercultural Preaching*. Oxford: Regents Park College Oxford, 2021.

Black Majority Churches

Adedibu, Babatunde. *Coat of Many Colours: The Origin, Growth, Distinctiveness and Contributions of Black Majority Churches to British Christianity*. London: Wisdom Summit, 2012.

Aldred, Joe and Keno Ogbo, Eds. *The Black Church in the 21st Century*. London: Darton, Longman & Todd, 2010.

Beckford, Robert. *Jesus is Dread: Black Theology and Black Culture in Britain*. London: Darton, Longman & Todd, 1998.

Beckford, Robert. *Dread and Pentecostalism: A Political Theology for the Black Church in Britain*. London: SPCK, 2000.

Chike, Chigor. *African Christianity in Britain: Diaspora, Doctrines and Dialogue*. Milton Keynes: Author House, 2007.

Francis, Roy. *Windrush and the Black Pentecostal Church in Britain*. Croydon: Filament Publishing, 2020.

Gerloff, Roswith. *A Plea for Black British Theologies*. Frankfurt: Peter Lang, 1992.

Olofinjana, Israel, Ed. *African Voices: Towards African British Theologies*. Carlisle: Langham Global Library, 2017.

Smith, I.O. with Wendy Green. *An Ebony Cross: Being a Black Christian in Britain Today*. London: HarperCollins, 1989.

Sturge, Mark. *Look What the Lord Has Done!: An Exploration of Black Christian Faith in Britain*. Bletchley: Scripture Union, 2005.

Leadership

Coleman, Kate. *Leadership in a Racialised World*. New Wine, 2021. https://www.youtube.com/watch?v=Bjhj1iiR-TI (Accessed March 2021).

Coleman, Kate. *7 Deadly Sins of Women in Leadership: Overcome Self-Defeating Behavior in Work and Ministry*. Birmingham: Next Leadership, 2010.

Thompson, Phyllis, Ed. *Challenges of Black Pentecostal Leadership in the 21st Century*. London: SPCK, 2013.

Climate Justice

Christian Aid, 'Our Prophetic Journey towards Climate Justice', https://www.christianaid.org.uk/resources/get-involved/our-prophetic-journey-towards-climate-justice-pdf (Accessed March 2021).

About the Author

Rev. Dr. Israel Oluwole Olofinjana (Ph.D.) is the new Director of the One People Commission of the Evangelical Alliance. He is an ordained and accredited Baptist minister and has led two multi-ethnic Baptist churches and an independent charismatic church. He is the founding director of the Centre for Missionaries from the Majority World, a mission network initiative that provides cross-cultural training to reverse missionaries in Britain. Israel is an Honorary Research Fellow at the Queen's Foundation for Ecumenical Theological Education in Birmingham and is on the Advisory Group on Race and Theology of the Society for the Study of Theology (SST). He is a consultant to the Executive Team of Lausanne Europe, advising them on matters related to diaspora ministries in Europe. He is on the Christian Aid Working Group of Black Majority Church leaders, exploring the intersection of climate justice and racial justice.

He is a Yoruba Nigerian coming from a Pentecostal background. He holds a B.A. (Hons) in Religious Studies from the University of Ibadan, Nigeria and M.Th. from Carolina University of Theology (CUT). Israel's Ph.D. thesis, through his publications, has been to develop African British Theology, exploring African identity through Intercultural Missiology and Public Theology. He has published several books, including editing *World Christianity in Western Europe: Diasporic Identity, Narratives and Missiology* (2020), *African Voices: Towards African British Theologies* (2017), *Turning the Tables on Mission: Stories of Christians from the Global South in the UK* (2013) and co-editing *Encountering London: London Baptists in the 21ˢᵗ Century* (2015). He is the author of *Reverse in Ministry and Missions: Africans in the Dark Continent of Europe* (2010), *20 Pentecostal Pioneers in Nigeria* (2011) and *Partnership in Mission: A Black Majority Church Perspective on Mission and Church Unity* (2015). He is happily married to Lucy Olofinjana, who is the Senior Media and Communications Officer for Churches Together in England (CTE). They are blessed with two children, Iyanuoluwa (meaning God's miracle) and Ireti (meaning hope).

Centre for Missionaries from the Majority World

Centre for Missionaries from the Majority World is a network/training hub that aims to prepare, equip and encourage pastors and missionaries from the Majority World in Britain as well as help indigenous British Christians and churches understand Christians from the South.

Missionary Identity

We are a collective of missionaries and leaders from the Majority World who see Europe as a mission field and therefore want to contextualise our mission and help others to engage in intercultural mission in the British/European context. This mission also drives our vision and shapes it.

Mission

The centre prepares, equips and encourages pastors and missionaries from the Majority World in Britain and other parts of Europe to understand the post-modern secular context of European societies and culture.

A second objective is encouraging southern scholarship and publications through books, journals and other forms of academic materials. This is to develop a strong theology of mission that is practical and to help the next generation of mission practitioners from the Majority World.

Another objective is helping British indigenous Christians and church leaders understand the mission and theology of Christians from the Majority World so as to improve relationships between both of them. Part of the learning is helping British indigenous Christians understand the background of these missionaries.

The centre helps guide pastors and missionaries who are interested in church planting to find out where a church plant might be needed. This is to avoid several churches being planted in the same proximity. This involves networking and research to make information available in terms of where churches, mission initiatives or projects might be best needed. This is to avoid competition and waste of resources that could be diverted to the right places at the right time.

Lastly, the centre directors are mission consultants who can be contacted on a number of issues related to Diaspora Mission, building a multicultural church, intercultural mission, currents and trends in World Christianity, whole-life discipleship, evangelism, mission training and post-colonial theologies.

Vision

Training, Consultation and Research

Training/Equipping

- Who? Reverse missionaries, people, organisations and churches working in the area of Diaspora Mission and indigenous white Christians and churches
- How? Through one-day conferences, webinars, seminars, short courses, invitations from mission organisations and churches and collaboration with other training centres and institutions
- Areas covered: Reverse Mission, Diaspora Mission, Developing Multicultural Churches, Cross-Cultural Mission and World Christianity

Mission Consultation

- Who? Mission organisations, theological colleges, Church denominations and networks
- How? One-to-one consultation, networking, collaborative consultations
- Areas: We have a range of expertise in different areas of mission, theology and church traditions; therefore we could cover the following: Diaspora Mission, Reverse Mission, Multicultural Christianity, World Christianity, Partnership in Mission, Church Planting, Leadership Development

Research

- Who? Our research is to benefit Majority World Christians in Britain as well as indigenous white organisations who

want to understand the dynamics of Diaspora Mission in the twenty-first century
- How? Through commissioned research projects, published monographs (books), edited volumes, CMMW blog (already online!), research papers and collaborative research with other research centres
- Areas of research: Reverse Mission, Diaspora Mission, World Christianity, Multicultural Christianity, Contextual Theologies, Pentecostal Studies and Practical Theology

History

The centre started with a conversation around reverse mission and the need to network, train and equip Majority World missionaries and pastors in Britain. In attendance were four of us: Peter Oyugi, Tayo Arikawe, Harvey Kwiyani and Israel Olofinjana. The team has since grown into seven of us, now including Usha Reifsnider, Samuel Cueva and Brenda Amondi. In October 2013 the Centre, as well as a book resource (*Turning the Tables on Mission: Stories of Christians from the Global South in Britain*), was launched at the Evangelical Alliance headquarters by Steve Clifford (former General Director). We had about seventy church leaders from across the country in attendance.

In March–May 2014 we had Missional Conversations with a few mission leaders and theologians once a month for a period of three months. This was held at Brockley Baptist Church, hosted by the then pastor, Rev. Dave Mahon, and his wife Rev. Michele Mahon.

In September 2014, in partnership with Spurgeon's College, South Asian Forum (SAF), South Asian Concern (SAC) and One People Commission, we had a one-day conference exploring the theme 'Partnership in Mission'. Rev. Yemi Adedeji (Director of One People Commission), Pastor Celia Apeagyei (Founder of Rehoboth Foundation) and Dr. Roger Standing (former Principal of Spurgeon's College) were speakers at this pioneering conference.

In March 2015, in partnership with the Ethiopian Christian Fellowship Church at King's Cross and through the effort of Rev. Dr. Girma Bishaw and the Evangelical Alliance, we had another one-day conference exploring multicultural churches. Speakers were Mark Sturge, Rev. David Wise and Rev. Michele Mahon.

In November 2015, we had a Pastor's Brunch for about fifteen church leaders representing the Majority World. This was hosted by the Ethiopian Christian Fellowship Church at King's Cross.

In July 2016, we partnered with Birmingham Churches Together and the Queen's Foundation for Ecumenical Theological Education in organising a one-day conference themed 'Every Tribe, Nation and Language: Growing Multi-Ethnic Churches'. Rev. Dr. Steve Hollinghurst (Church Army), Dr. Tani Omideyi (Temple of Praise Church) and Dr. Harvey Kwiyani (CMS then, now Liverpool Hope University) were speakers.

In June 2017 at Bristol, we partnered with the Church of God of Prophecy, Grace Evangelistic Ministries and St. Mark Baptist Church, Bristol, we had a day conference with the theme 'Every Tribe, Nation and Language: Growing Multi-Ethnic Multicultural

Churches'. Rev. Dr. Kate Coleman (Next Leadership) and Bishop Ray Veira (Church of God of Prophecy) were speakers.

In October 2017, we partnered with London City Mission and organised a day conference with the theme 'African and Caribbean Theologies'. The event also saw the launch of the book *African Voices: Towards African British Theologies*. Rev. Wale Hudson-Roberts, Racial Justice Enabler for Baptists Together, moderated the event while Dr. Dulcie Dixon McKenzie (Queen's Foundation), Dr. Eben Adu, Rev. Chigor Chike and Rev. Valerie Taiwo spoke about their contributions to the book.

In March 2018, in conjunction with the Baptist Missionary Society (BMS) training centre in Birmingham, we organised a mission conference themed 'Mission and Migration'. Dr. Kang-San Tan, BMS General Director, Rev. Claire Ord and Rev. Mark Ord all spoke.

In October 2018, we worked with Sheffield Community Church to put together a mission conference themed 'World Christianity in Britain'. One of the exciting emerging themes that the conference addressed briefly was the issue of second-generation Africans in the diaspora. Dr. Anderson Moyo hosted us as the senior pastor of the church and also spoke on African Diaspora Christianity. We also had Dr. Emma Wild-Wood (Centre for the Study of World Christianity), Usha Reifsnider (Lausanne Europe and CMMW) and Dr. Samuel Cueva (Mission for the Third Millennium) speaking.

In June 2019, in partnership with All Nations Christian College, Global Connections and the Movement of African National

Initiatives (MANI), we organised a two-day mission consultation on 'The State of Diaspora Mission in the UK'. The keynote speaker was Dr. Joel Edwards CBE. Other speakers include Pastor Peter Rong (Spiritual Revival Baptist Church, Romania), Dr. Tani Omideyi (Temple of Praise Church, Liverpool), Usha Reifsnider (Lausanne Europe and CMMW), Dr. Girma Bishaw (Gratitude Initiative), Henry Lu (Chinese Overseas Christian Mission) and Louisa Evans (All Nations Christian College).

Currently some of the team members are working with Lausanne Europe as consultants serving in various teams towards a European consultation in Poland in October 2020, now postponed to November 2021. The theme of the consultation is 'Dynamic Gospel in a New Europe'.

CMMW, in partnership with Faiths Forum (an online theological conversation) and Missio Africanus, organised the launch of two books: *World Christianity in Western Europe: Diasporic Identities, Narratives and Missiology*, edited by Israel Olofinjana and *Multicultural Kingdom: Ethnic Diversity, Mission and the Church*, authored by Dr. Harvey Kwiyani in July 2020 on Facebook Live.

CMMW Team

Dr. Samuel Cueva is a Peruvian missiologist whose Ph.D. explored partnership in mission between Western churches and Latin American churches. He is a mission consultant with an expertise in Reciprocal Collaboration Mission Theology. He is the founder and President of Mission for the Third Millennium, which organises conferences on Global Mission. He is also a member of the Evangelical Alliance, One People Commission and Latin American Core Group. He speaks at various national and international conferences, publishes articles in different journals and is the author of *Mission Partnership in Creative Tension* (2015). He currently lectures on Mission Theology at the University of Roehampton, London. He is the founder of Latin American Pastors Fellowship in London.

Dr. Harvey Kwiyani is the newly appointed CEO of Global Connections and teaches part-time at CMS college. He was a former lecturer in African Christianity and Theology at Liverpool Hope University. He has spent over ten years working as both a scholar and a practitioner in missions in Europe and North America. He graduated with a Ph.D. from Luther Seminary in 2012, having researched the theological implications of the missionary work of Africans in North America. Harvey has now published some of his research findings in his book, *Sent Forth: African Missionary Work in the West* (Orbis Books, 2014). He formerly taught Missions, Leadership and African Studies at Birmingham Christian College and at Church Mission Society (CMS) in Oxford. He is also Research Fellow at the Cuddesdon Study Centre at Ripon College, Cuddesdon. His current book is *Multicultural Kingdom: Ethnic Diversity, Mission and the Church* (2020).

Peter Oyugi hails from Kenya and currently serves as Movement of African National Initiatives (MANI) European co-ordinator and on the leadership of Majority World Christian Leaders. He previously worked for African Inland Mission (AIM) and served as the pastor of an evangelical church in London. After initially studying Electrical and Communications Engineering in Kenya, Peter later graduated with an M.A. in Missions from Redcliffe College (University of Gloucestershire) and an M.B.A. (Leadership) from the University of Liverpool. He regularly teaches the Bible at IFES conferences in English-speaking Africa. He also serves on the councils of Global Connections and All Nations Christian College. Peter has a passion for cross-cultural mission that has grown out of being exposed to different cultures from childhood. His father is Kenyan and mother Finnish. He is an avid sports lover and takes a keen interest in African politics. Peter is married to Cecilia and they have two daughters.

Tayo Arikawe is currently the International Director of Langham Partnership. Before that he was the Director of Ministries at London City Mission (LCM). He is an ordained minister, a missionary and Bible teacher. One of his interests is reverse/inverse mission, with a view to building multicultural churches that will reach out to the lost in the continent of Europe. He is the International Director of Grace Evangelistic Ministries Europe (GEM), a non-denominational Bible-teaching missionary organisation whose first priority is to take the gospel of grace to a lost and dying world. The ministry operates in over sixty countries of the world. Tayo completed an MTh from the University of Chester via the Wales Evangelical School of Theology. He also holds a B.Sc. in Geology and Mineral Science from the University of Ilorin, Nigeria. On a good day, he is at the gym doing bodily exercise. He is married to Calista and they are blessed with one son, Mekus. Tayo is currently working on a Ph.D. in Biblical Studies at the University of Gloucestershire.

Usha Reifsnider is British Gujarati from the West Midlands. She and husband Matt served as missionaries with Go To Nations since 1988. They spent ten years in a Muslim country ministering to refugees and migrant workers. They also serve as mission strategists with the International Learning Center, an English language school and church-planting programme for international communities in the USA. She formerly served as the Church Relations Manager at South Asian Concern (SAC) and Programme Co-ordinator at South Asian Forum (SAF) at the Evangelical Alliance. Usha holds an M.A. from the University of Chester and is currently studying for a Ph.D. at the Oxford Centre for Mission Studies researching Diaspora Mission. She is on the executive and co-ordination team of Lausanne European 20/21 Conversation and Gathering and speaks at national conferences such as Spring Harvest.

Rev. Dr. Israel Oluwole Olofinjana is the Director of One People Commission of the Evangelical Alliance. He is an ordained and accredited Baptist minister previously the pastor of Woolwich Central Baptist Church South East London. He previously pastored Crofton Park Baptist Church (2007–2011) and Catford Community Church (2011–2013).

He is Nigerian, coming from a Pentecostal background. He holds a B.A. (Hons) in Religious Studies from the University of Ibadan, Nigeria and a M.Th. from Carolina University of Theology (CUT).

Israel is the editor of *World Christianity in Western Europe: Diasporic Identities, Narratives and Missiology* (2020), *African Voices: Towards African British Theologies* (2017), *Turning the Tables on Mission: Stories of Christians from the Global South in the UK* (2013) and author of *Reverse in Ministry and Missions: Africans in the Dark Continent of Europe* (2010), *20 Pentecostal Pioneers in Nigeria* (2011) and *Partnership in Mission: A Black Majority Church Perspective on Mission and Church Unity* (2015). He is an Honorary Research Fellow at the Queen's Foundation for Ecumenical Theological Education in Birmingham. He is currently doing some work with Christian Aid on Black Majority Churches and Climate Justice. He is also on the Executive Team of Lausanne Europe. He is happily married to Lucy, who works at Churches Together in England as their Senior Media and Communications Officer. They are blessed with Iyanuoluwa and Ireti.

Brenda Ouma is a missionary and a church planter from Kenya. She formerly served in the capacity of a Community and Youth Worker, under the Church of England, at St. Luke's Earls Court, in London.

Brenda has served as a missionary with Nairobi Chapel Church since 2014. For the first two years she worked under the Youth Ministry as the Creative Service Co-ordinator while undergoing leadership training geared towards church planting and pastoral ministry. Prior to this, in 2011 she served in the Nairobi Youth Diocese, in the Anglican Church of Kenya. Her involvement was in missions to secondary and university students.

In 2016, Brenda, together with a team of seven others, planted a church in the south of Nairobi – Nairobi Chapel South Church. She was tasked with starting a children's ministry, which she did excellently, having raised and nurtured a team of leaders to continue the work. In September 2017 she pioneered the Youth Ministry at St. Luke's Earls Court.

Brenda holds a B.A. in Interior Design from the University of Nairobi and an M.A. in Christian Leadership, with a focus on theology, culture and the arts, at St. Mellitus College. Her desire is to be used by God to draw people across all cultures to Jesus and share in the joy of salvation. Her passions revolve around people, leadership and the creative arts.

Contact us

israelolofinjana@yahoo.co.uk

Centre for Missionaries from the Majority World

www.cmmw.org.uk